" Faith makes things
possible, not easy."
Thank you for sharing
our family's journey
Fondly,
Nancy Galusha

The Ribbon Is Black for a Reason

How Melanoma Changed My Life in Four Short Months

Nancy A. Midey Galusha

authorHOUSE®

AuthorHouse™
1663 Liberty Drive
Bloomington, IN 47403
www.authorhouse.com
Phone: 1-800-839-8640

Published by AuthorHouse 2/21/2013

ISBN: 978-1-4817-1878-3 (sc)
ISBN: 978-1-4817-1877-6 (e)

Library of Congress Control Number: 2013903129

"I'm Screwed."

"This is *not* mastoiditis," the head doctor of the ear, nose, and throat team at Strong Memorial Hospital announced on July 20, 2010, in the emergency room. "I'm very sorry, Mr. Galusha. If this were mastoiditis, you would have a raging ear infection. We don't see any sign of an ear infection. This is most likely a tumor. You have a very large tumor in your pelvic region as well. We were able to look at your CT scan from yesterday. We can't say for sure, but, considering that you have tumors in two different locations, it's most likely cancer."

I literally felt the floor fall away from my feet at the sound of the doctor's preliminary diagnosis. I began to shake uncontrollably. Jerry glanced over at me and said without emotion, "I'm screwed."

My knees were knocking, and my teeth were chattering when a kind and observant nurse placed a heated blanket around my shoulders. It was 90 degrees outside, and, although it was very warm in the tiny, overcrowded cubicle that contained my husband's emergency room bed, I felt a chill that I had never felt before. I was stone cold.

Getting to this point was a short trip. On the weekend of June 9, 2010, Jerry mentioned that he had a headache. Throughout that week, he described it as a pain in the back of the right side of his head that radiated down to his shoulder. When he mentioned the pain to a friend at work, his friend told him that his skin in that area was red. By the end of the week, he was alarmed enough to go to the doctor.

"You're having muscle spasms," the physician's assistant said. He then prescribed a muscle relaxer and told Jerry to return in a week if he didn't feel better.

Jerry nursed that pain for a little over a month. Some days it seemed slightly better, and other days it was worse. Jerry took an alarming amount of ibuprofen each day in an attempt to make this headache go away ... but it didn't go away. I found out later that Jerry had also taken some pain medicine leftover from some old dental work, but even that didn't provide lasting relief.

I nagged like any wife does when her husband clearly needs to see a doctor and won't take the time off from work to do it. I made him change his contact lenses in the hope that eye strain was causing his headaches. He switched from sleeping on two pillows to one to rule out neck strain. We addressed all of the obvious causes of a headache to no avail. Finally on the weekend of July 14, I said, "If you don't go to the doctor Monday, don't come home from work." Of course I didn't mean it literally, but I knew that this was the threat that would give Jerry the motivation to take the day off and go back to the doctor. He could honestly call his boss and say, "Nancy's *making* me go back to the doctor." And that's exactly what he did.

Bad News Always Comes Back Quickly

On Monday, July 16, 2010, Jerry called the doctor's office and made an appointment for later that morning. The same physician's assistant saw him and said that he thought that Jerry had pulled a ligament in the back of his head and that it was taking longer than usual to heal, but, to be on the safe side, he wanted Jerry to have an MRI that afternoon. While I drove Jerry to the hospital for his MRI, I felt unusually nervous about the speed in which this test had been scheduled. The MRI took almost an hour, and when it was over we made a quick stop at the shoe store. At 5:33 p.m., Jerry took his phone out of his pocket and noticed a missed call from the doctor's office. The message waved the first of many red flags.

"Mr. Galusha, we have some results from your MRI. I'll be in the office until 5:30. Give me a call before then." Jerry dialed quickly, but everybody had already left for the day.

"Jerry, I don't mean to be negative, or to scare you,

but only bad news comes back this fast," I said. We had only left the hospital forty-five minutes earlier.

As soon as the doctor's office opened the next morning, Jerry was on the phone. The physician's assistant explained that they had found a mass in the mastoid area of Jerry's skull. He told Jerry that he needed to see a neurologist at Rochester General Hospital on Thursday. The two days leading up to that appointment were emotionally grueling. In my heart, I knew that something terrible was looming, but I tried to be somewhat positive. Common sense told me not to tell Jerry, "I told you to go back to the doctor sooner." To this day, I'm very grateful that I didn't resort to that kind of chastising, as I discovered, not much later, that it wouldn't have changed a single thing.

I visited my mother that evening to prepare her for bad news. My mother adored Jerry. He was a second son to her. She tried to convince me, and convince herself, that this was nothing more than some sort of strange infection and would be cleared up with a good old fashioned dose of antibiotics. My instincts told me differently. I tried to be very honest with her and explained that the word "mass" is just a synonym for "tumor," but she wasn't ready to hear it, so I left her house knowing that I'd failed to prepare her for what I felt was going to be earth-shattering news.

On Thursday, Jerry and I met the first of several neurologists that would be involved with my husband's health care in the following months. He looked at Jerry's MRI for quite a while but then admitted that the mastoid was not an area that he was very familiar with, so he asked us to go downstairs to have a CT scan of

Jerry's chest, abdomen, and pelvis. He prescribed this scan because of Jerry's previous melanoma thirteen years before. "Let's rule out anything really bad," the doctor had told us. If only it had been that easy. That doctor scheduled an appointment for Jerry the following day with a colleague.

History: Summer, 1997

A mole on the back of Jerry's left calf had changed. It had grown larger and had changed in color from brown to black. The sides of the mole had also gotten ragged in appearance; they were not smooth like they had been before. I noticed it when the weather got warmer and he was wearing shorts more often. I commented on it several times and asked him to see our dermatologist, but he brushed it off as a waste of time. One evening I took my mom to a friend's yard sale. The woman who was having the sale was a friend of a friend. "Did Angela tell you about my cancer scare?" she asked. She showed me a long, fresh scar on her leg and explained that she'd had a malignant mole removed and told me how dangerously close she'd been to being in "real trouble." Her description of her own mole also described Jerry's mole. The very next day I called our dermatologist's office and made an appointment for Jerry. He had no choice now. I was forcing him to go. He was angry with me because it was a busy time at work, and he thought that his boss would be angry with him for taking a day off. The dermatologist took one look at Jerry's mole and sent him directly to a plastic surgeon in Canandaigua. The plastic surgeon removed the mole that day. A couple of days later, he called our house with the results of the biopsy. Jerry wasn't home, so I took the call.

"Your husband's mole was malignant, Mrs. Galusha. Do you understand how serious melanoma can be?"

I was defensive and replied, "Dr. E., you don't realize that I'm the one who made my husband's appointment in the first place? He wouldn't have done anything about the mole if I hadn't made him!" Why did doctors always blame wives for their husbands stubbornness? I fumed.

The melanoma diagnosis brought with it a series of scans and blood tests. At first Jerry had to see the dermatologist every three months, and then every six months, but in time he only had to attend skin check appointments once a year. During those appointments, the doctor would check his lymph nodes and existing moles. Year after year, the doctor gave him a clean bill of health. Insurance companies don't allow further scanning after a patient has been cancer-free for two years unless there is reason to believe that it's necessary. It sickens me today to think that my husband's growing cancer might have been detected much earlier if scans had been required or available beyond the two-year mark.

It Just Keeps Getting Worse

Jerry's pain worsened every day. By the time we got to the second neurologist on Friday, Jerry was extremely uncomfortable even though he was taking strong pain medications and steroids to reduce the inflammation of the mass. Before we got on the thruway, I had to pull over at a gas station so he could vomit. Jerry barely spoke to me as we waited in the doctor's office. He rested his head on my shoulder and closed his eyes. This doctor actually gave us a glimmer of hope. He looked at the MRI and said that he thought that Jerry had mastoiditis, an infection in the mastoid area of the skull. According to this doctor, it could be cured with IV antibiotics. He instructed us to go to Strong Memorial Hospital's emergency room because mastoiditis could lead to meningitis, and Jerry needed to start an IV antibiotic immediately. He called the ear, nose, and throat team of doctors at the ER to ask that Jerry be seen as soon as possible and asked that they look at his MRI and CT scan results from the day before to make a final determination of Jerry's diagnosis.

As is often the case with emergency rooms, it was two

or three hours before Jerry was actually lying on a bed. The head ENT doctor and his team examined Jerry and then excused themselves to review his MRI and CT scan results. Upon their return, their faces told a very grim story: "This is not mastoiditis, Mr. Galusha. You have two tumors. One is a skull-based tumor. That is the one that is causing all of your pain. The other is a very large tumor in your pelvic region. We're sorry to deliver bad news, but these tumors are most likely cancerous, and the fact that you have a history of melanoma makes it very likely that your melanoma has metastasized. We'll get you a room in the hospital and start getting biopsies as soon as possible."

The head ENT doctor told me later in the summer that the second neurologist had known that Jerry's mass was a malignant tumor but didn't have the heart to tell us in his office. He left it up to the ear, nose, and throat team instead. I've never forgiven him for giving us false hope. Those few hours of respite were a cruel trick.

I stayed with Jerry in the emergency room until he was just about to fall asleep. I learned later that he wasn't moved to a hospital room until 4:00 a.m. During the next week, doctors took a lot of biopsies and tried to get his pain under control.

The "C" Word

I called my sister, Joan, from the parking lot before I left the hospital. Sobbing, I blurted out to her, "Jerry has cancer!" I didn't need a biopsy to tell me the definitive, terrifying news. There was no doubt in my mind that Jerry had cancer. My sister and brother wanted to drive to Rochester, an hour away from their home, to meet me and drive me home. "*No!* I want to go home now," I cried. "I can't wait an hour in this parking lot," I said as I drove away from the hospital and from my husband, *the cancer patient*.

When I arrived home, my mother, sister, and brother were already sitting in my living room. I immediately fell into my sister's arms. She'd lost her husband a little over three years before in a car accident. How could this be happening again? I told them what I knew so far—that Jerry had two tumors and that because he'd had a malignant mole years ago, it was likely that the melanoma had metastasized and caused these tumors. All three offered to stay with me that night. I didn't want anyone to distract me from my thoughts. I knew that I needed to be alone.

Of course, I didn't sleep much. There was too much to take in, and I didn't even know where to begin. Not only was I worried about my husband of nineteen years and myself, but we had two children away at camp who didn't even know that their father was in the hospital. Danny, our seventeen-year-old, had left for camp three weeks earlier to work as a resident counselor. He only knew that his dad had been having headaches, but I doubted that he had given it much thought. His father's work often caused muscle pain, small injuries, and discomfort. Phillip, our thirteen-year-old, attended the camp where Danny worked. They were both scheduled to come home the next day, Saturday, and return to camp on Sunday. In that short time, I would have to tell them that their father had two tumors and that they were most likely malignant. It was the most awful task I'd ever been given. Unfortunately, the tasks got more horrific as time went on.

Telling Our Sons

I drove to Livonia the next morning in an exhausted daze. When I arrived at the camp, I saw Danny first and tried my best to act as if nothing was wrong. Danny would arrive home later with his cousin, Tricia, who was also a camp counselor, because the counselors stayed later than the campers did to clean the cabins. I didn't want something as heavy as a preliminary cancer diagnosis to distract their driving. I could wait to tell him.

Phillip and I got into the van, and he excitedly rambled on about the experiences he'd had that week. He played a CD of the music that the camp band made all the way home. The music was annoying at best, given my state of mind, but I tolerated it for Phillip's sake. We stopped quickly at a fast food restaurant to get him something to eat. I couldn't eat a bite. I was nauseous knowing that I had terrible information that the boys didn't even suspect. Our lives had changed immensely in the short time since they'd been gone, and they were completely unaware of it.

When we stepped into the house, cool from the air

conditioning, I said, "Phillip, will you sit down for a minute? I have to talk to you about something." I felt my throat choke up with emotion that I couldn't control, but I didn't want to scare him.

He asked, "Who died?" Unfortunately, life's experiences had already taught Phillip that when we asked him to sit down in a serious tone of voice, it usually meant that something tragic had happened. The year before, when Phillip returned from camp, we had informed him that his beloved cat, Stormy, had been hit by a car and had to be put down. I would have given anything to have the same kind of news to share. A cat can be replaced, but his father's illness was going to turn his world upside down.

I said, "No one died, Phillip. But Dad is in the hospital in Rochester. Remember the headache that he couldn't get rid of? Well, he had some tests done this past week, and just yesterday the doctors found a tumor on Dad's skull and another in his pelvis. The doctors told us that these tumors are probably cancer, but we don't know that for sure yet."

The tears came quickly and freely. When I was able to get my emotions under control, I foolishly asked Phillip if he was okay. He turned to me when he was able to find his voice and said, "I'm just thinking about what it's gonna be like without Dad." I had been wondering the same thing since I'd heard the word "cancer" the day before. I'll never be able to explain why, but from that very moment, I positively knew that my husband would die quickly. I never felt hope, and I never felt that we had much time, and I was right on both accounts.

Phillip and I cried, and we held each other for a long time. Eventually, he went into his bedroom to lie down.

I checked on him frequently, and we hugged many times that day. We had been thrust into an entirely new life. We had been dealt a huge blow, and we felt and looked like struck people.

About the time that I expected Danny to pull in, he called from a shopping mall and informed me that it was going to take longer than expected to get home because he was buying his girlfriend's birthday gifts. I kept my voice from shaking and told him to be careful and that I'd see him when he got home. Finally, at about 3:30 p.m., Danny bounded into the house, full of life, tanned and with hair longer than it had ever been before, and dropped a duffel bag filled with his dirty laundry at his feet. He was handsome and had quite literally become a man in those weeks he'd been away from home for the first time. My heart broke thinking that I had to ruin his special day with Lea. He had plans to spend time with her, and what I was going to tell him would spoil everything. Although I hated myself for it, I hated cancer even more.

"Danny, would you sit down? There's some stuff that I need to talk to you about."

He sat down tentatively. He could tell by my demeanor that it was serious.

"What's wrong, Mom?"

"Honey, do you remember that Dad had some headaches before you left for camp?"

"Yeah," he said cautiously. He knew something bad was coming, I could tell by his expression and by the way his whole body tensed up. He was preparing for a blow.

"Well, the headaches got worse, and this past week Dad had a lot of tests done, and just yesterday the doctors told us that Dad has two tumors. One is on the base of his skull and one is in his pelvis. Not his brain, Dan. Dad does *not* have a brain tumor. It's on the base of his skull in an area called the mastoid." For some reason, I had to make sure that my sons understood that their father didn't have a brain tumor. Somehow, in my confused thoughts, that made this news slightly less awful and more palatable.

Tears came again, and this time, they were body-wracking, gulping tears. I had broken my children's hearts that day. No one should ever have to deliver such frightening, devastating news to two boys who adored their father as much as my sons did. I have literally never hated myself so much in my life. How could a mother hurt her children like that?

Phillip had come into the room and could tell by his brother's strong emotions that I had just delivered the news. The three of us took turns holding each other as we tried to convince ourselves and each other that many cancers could be cured or controlled. "Let's not think the worst until we hear differently," we all agreed.

Now We're a Cancer Family

Although Danny initially asked to be taken, I didn't drive the boys to the hospital that day. If memory serves me well, my brother and sister went to Rochester and kept Jerry company for a few hours. I was too tired from the sleepless night before to be able to drive safely, and the boys were exhausted from camp. I promised them that I'd take them both to the hospital on our way back to camp the next day. Danny had to make arrangements to be a little late for work on Sunday. We had already paid for Phillip to attend camp for two consecutive weeks with just this one day break in between. I told Phillip that I wouldn't make him return to camp for his second week, but I outlined all of the positives about going back to camp. He would be near Danny, and I'd be spending every day an hour away at the hospital while his dad was having biopsies and tests. In the end, Phillip made the choice to go back to camp for the second week.

That evening, my family gathered at my house in an effort to support us. There truly is strength in numbers. Sadly, we had experience with trauma. As I mentioned earlier, three years before Jerry's tumors appeared on MRI and CT scans, my sister's husband, Jim, was killed instantly in a tragic car accident. He was alive one minute and gone the next. It happened just that fast. My family knew what to do in an emergency. We'd seen each other through the most excruciating experience we'd ever had to endure, but fate was dealing us another blow much too soon. My nieces enveloped my sons in their love, humor, and support that night. My brother, sister, and mother did the same for me. It was enough to help us take our first baby steps into the world of terminal illness.

I don't remember when or how decisions were made that night, but my mother and sister took the boys' dirty camp laundry and washed it for them, bought Phillip snacks to take back to camp, and delivered everything to my house before we left the next day. It was a prelude to all that they would do for me that summer. I never once cleaned my own house from the day of Jerry's cancer diagnosis until late in August. It was always miraculously clean when I'd return from a doctor's appointment or a radiation treatment. My loved ones took amazing care of me and my family during Jerry's illness.

On the way to the hospital the next day, the boys and I tried to be positive. I knew that they were nervous about seeing their father in a large, unfamiliar hospital, hooked up to IVs and in whatever condition we were going to find him in, but when we arrived, Jerry was pain-free thanks to strong narcotics, and he was in good spirits. We had a pleasant visit, and it was good for the boys to spend time with their dad. They felt hopeful that their father would fight his cancer and get well. Even though I had my doubts, I wouldn't take their hope away.

That wouldn't have been fair before we had more facts. A doctor came into Jerry's room and Danny asked many intelligent, thoughtful questions. I could tell that we were all clinging to the most positive of responses and letting go of the negative ones in a desperate attempt to will Jerry back to health.

I dropped the boys off at camp that afternoon and told them to relax and enjoy the week as much as possible. Danny vowed to call every night for an update and then go to Phillip's cabin to deliver any news that I was able to give him. Danny continued to call or text me or Jerry, and often both of us, every night for the rest of the summer. His communications were peppered with advice for his father. He always told Jerry to make sure that he walked every day and to eat well and stay hydrated. I think that he tried to believe that these simple strategies would help his father stay strong enough to overcome cancer. What he didn't seem to understand or want to comprehend was that cancer isn't just an illness—it's a disease, and it's often deadly.

The Beginning of the Cancer Story

After I fed and dropped the boys off at camp that afternoon, I returned to the hospital to spend some more time with Jerry. Our friends Lori and Rick were visiting Jerry when I arrived. We had a nice visit and Lori, Rick, and I all left together an hour or so later. In the parking garage, they commented that Jerry looked great and that they had high hopes for a complete recovery. I turned to them solemnly and informed them that if this truly was metastasized melanoma, there was little chance of a positive outcome. They looked shocked that I was preparing for my husband's death, but I knew from the preliminary diagnosis and from the doctors' grim faces that this was not going to have a happy ending. No one else had been in the emergency room with me, Jerry, and the doctors when they told us that Jerry's cancer was probably metastasized, malignant melanoma. Those five sad faces said it all.

In the next two weeks, a lot happened and none of it was good. Jerry's cancer was positively diagnosed as stage four metastasized, malignant melanoma. Thirteen years is an incredibly long period of time for melanoma to travel through the body, growing tumors all the way up to the skull, but we learned that's exactly what had happened. A PET scan showed that Jerry had cancer throughout his body, including his spine, left shoulder, hips, lungs, kidneys, etc. Every time I saw a doctor's name on my caller ID, I felt sick to my stomach, because the news was never hopeful, and I was the person who had to deliver it to Jerry. There were a few times in those early days that doctors alluded to his negative prognosis in front of Jerry, but he was usually in such tremendous pain that he didn't hear it or he simply didn't understand their complicated medical jargon. The fact is he didn't ask a lot of questions about his prognosis. I don't think he really wanted to know … because, he really *did* know.

Uncontrollable Pain

During the first month after his diagnosis, Jerry had two separate week-long stays at Strong Memorial Hospital in an attempt to get his pain under control. He was sent home with what seemed a toxic number of narcotics. He spent several days vomiting even simple water and juice, due to his inability to adjust to the high doses. It seemed that the medications never really controlled or eliminated his pain; they just knocked him out so he'd sleep through it. As soon as he'd wake up, we were fighting to gain control over the pain all over again.

Finally, after one particularly bad day, I insisted that we go to the emergency room. I knew that Jerry was dehydrated, and that his pain was too intense to keep him home any longer. Upon entering the emergency room with Jerry in a wheelchair and a wastepaper basket between his legs in case he had to vomit again, I said aloud to the receptionist, a total stranger, "This is my husband, Gerard Galusha. He has a skull-based tumor. He is being treated for malignant melanoma." I had finally spoken the words. I had told a complete stranger that my husband had cancer, and the walls didn't crumble … but I did. After they took Jerry into triage, I went into the ladies bathroom and sobbed, cursing the words that I'd just spoken, afraid that it had upset Jerry. I discovered shortly after that I had no need to worry about Jerry's feelings. His pain was so terrible that he was yelling at everyone who got near him, demanding attention and medication. He got everything he asked for.

After being seen by the doctor on call that evening, Jerry was admitted to the hospital and kept overnight. It was the first decent night's sleep that I'd had since I brought Jerry home from his last stay at Strong Memorial Hospital. The responsibility of taking care of him was exhausting, but even though I was very tired, I didn't sleep well at night. I heard every noise that Jerry made and waited for the vomiting, moaning, and calling out in his sleep. When he was admitted, I gave that responsibility to the doctors and nurses at Geneva General Hospital. As a matter of fact, the emergency room doctor had first told me that if they got Jerry's pain under control, he'd send him home later that evening, but I insisted that he stay overnight. I knew that we'd just be fighting the same demon later. At least in the hospital they could continuously administer pain medication through an IV. That appeared to be the only real way we could give Jerry relief, as pills didn't do enough.

Radiation Begins

I arrived at the hospital early the next day, because I knew that I would need to make some important decisions. Jerry was supposed to go to a pain clinic in Rochester that day to have a nerve block in his head, but I was certain that he was too sick to make that appointment. It was clear that other arrangements would have to be made, and I was correct. We met Dr. F. that morning. He was genuine and caring and blunt. Dr. F. was the first person to ask me, "How the hell have you been taking care of him in this condition by yourself?" I'm grateful to this day that Dr. F. took over and advocated for us that morning. He made arrangements for Jerry to be transported to F. F. Thompson Hospital in Canandaigua via ambulance. The F. F. Thompson Hospital is affiliated with and connected to Sands Cancer Treatment Center, where we had agreed Jerry would begin radiation to his skull-based tumor. Radiation was supposed to begin on Thursday, but Dr. F. found out that the radiation mask that was specially made for Jerry was already at Sands waiting for his first treatment. Dr. F. assured me that Jerry would begin radiation that very day, Wednesday, and he did.

Sands Cancer Treatment Center became part of our daily lives. Jerry had fifteen radiation treatments on his skull, and the treatments did help, which was very fortunate, because melanoma is extremely resistant to traditional radiation and chemotherapy. The radiation shrunk Jerry's skull-based tumor enough to relieve the pain. Jerry remained a patient at F. F. Thompson during the first week of radiation. He was in too much pain to come home until they were able to truly get his pain under control with medication that didn't make him nauseous. The nurse who inserted Jerry's IV the first day made a comment that palliative care was much easier than curative care, because it was far less intense. Jerry didn't understand her comment, but I did. We weren't trying to cure Jerry; we were only trying to make him comfortable. I had to face the truth, and it was heartbreaking.

Making Adjustments

By this time I had quit my summer job as a librarian at a nearby summer school program. During my last week of employment, I received a frantic phone call from Jerry one day while I was working and he was still a patient at Strong Memorial Hospital. It was the day they were going to form his radiation mask, the medical professionals had asked him several questions that he didn't know how to answer. Because of pain and the high levels of medication, Jerry had difficulty answering their complicated questions. As a result, I needed to be more available, so going to work was out of the question. The summer school job was optional, but I worried constantly about going back to work full-time as a middle school librarian in the fall. How could I work when Jerry needed so much assistance? Just organizing his medication qualified as a full-time job. Also, each medication needed to be administered at the right time in order to maximize the little relief the drugs provided. This required precision and continual monitoring. It was a delicate balance, and we couldn't play with even five minutes, or Jerry's pain would be horribly intense until everything had time to kick in again. I created charts that we kept in the kitchen to monitor the time, dosage, and type of medication that I gave Jerry throughout the day. It truly was the only way to keep track of such a large number of medications. The stress and anxiety of Jerry's circumstances were all consuming. For two weeks after his diagnosis, I could feel my insides buzzing—that's the only way to describe it. It was as if an electrical current was constantly *on* in my body. It was a foreign, awful feeling.

A Short Reprieve

"Nothing is permanent in this world, not
even our troubles."—Charlie Chaplin

When Jerry was discharged from F. F. Thompson Hospital a week later, oral drugs were able to manage his pain better than ever before. Our family had better quality time together. Our daily trips to Sands Cancer Center became routine. The fifteen pounds that Jerry had initially lost were coming back on. Steroids made him very hungry, and we often had to stop for him to eat somewhere on the way home from radiation. We tried to have pleasant conversations, but it was strained. There was an eight-hundred-pound gorilla in the room, and its name was Death.

Jerry had worked for the Village of Seneca Falls for the past 10 years. He was proud of his work on the street department as his work enhanced the beauty of our historic village and made the roads safer to drive on during the winter months. Sadly, due to the poor economy and the perception that village government had gotten a bit out of hand, a vote was taken and the Village of Seneca Falls was going to dissolve. Jerry took the dissolution very hard as he felt that his work for the past 10 years had been unappreciated. However, there was a sizable amount of money left in the union account and Jerry had made arrangements for a clam bake with free food and beverages for each member. Those of us who weren't members but accompanied one only had to pay a small fee for unlimited food and drink. The week before, when Jerry was in the hospital, I never dreamed that he'd be able to attend his clam bake, but the day that it arrived he felt good enough to go. Jerry ate at least eight dozen clams, visited with friends from work, and simply enjoyed being one of the guys for the first time in weeks. I have such fond memories of that day.

When Prayers Change

"The unending paradox is that we do learn
through the pain."—Madeline L'Engle

When Jerry was first diagnosed with cancer, I went after
my rosary beads like any good Catholic, Italian woman
does. The ritual of praying the rosary was very comforting
to me, because this form of prayer didn't require me to
think. It was emotionless, which is exactly what I had
to offer at that time. I would simply recite the long-ago
memorized prayers while moving the smooth plastic
beads through my fingers and around my hands. I prayed
diligently, not only for Jerry but also for David T. and
Don A., who were battling progressive cancers at the
same time. I knew these men's wives personally, and I
could relate to the desperation in their voices when they
asked for prayers for their husbands. At first I thought
that asking for anything less than miracles for the three
men would be underestimating the power of God and
His ability to perform supernatural miracles. I'd pray as
many rosaries as I could each night before succumbing

to sleep. I was confusing quantity for quality. I prayed faithfully for the first few weeks. My prayers were the pleas of a child, and I knew that they were insulting my relationship with God. In my heart, I felt that God wanted to hear from me on a more personal level. I really needed to have an actual conversation with God, but I was afraid. The truth is I didn't believe for a second that I deserved the miracle I was asking for. Jerry *did*, but I didn't. Who was I to expect a cure for my husband when I'd been less than perfect my entire life? I am very aware of the fact that I can be extremely sarcastic and harsh. I use bad language and think less than stellar thoughts about many people. And those are just the sins that I can share here. There are many more. As much as I respect my Catholic upbringing, unfortunately, we Roman Catholics tend to believe that praying for something that could benefit ourselves is selfish; therefore, I made it very clear to God that my thoughts and prayers were strictly for Jerry, David, and Don. I found though, in time, that I wanted and needed to pray differently. I tried to just talk to God, but it's hard when you get silence instead of answers. Why couldn't God, just this one time, verbally respond to me?

I was alone one afternoon driving my van when the old Beatles song, "Let It Be" came on the radio. I had an epiphany. I know it was an epiphany and not just a thought, because I haven't had many epiphanies in my life, and I know the difference when one occurs. A thought or feeling comes and goes fairly quickly. An epiphany stays with you. You can easily conjure up the emotions you felt at the time long after they occurred. Those three simple words were the response that I'd been asking for from

God. "Let It Be" meant that I didn't need to tell God what to do, and I didn't have to know what the future held. I realized that what God expected of me was really very simple. He wanted me to stay out of His way and let him do what He had to do. Jerry had terminal cancer. I wasn't going to pray our way out of this one. I had to let it be. From that very moment on, I simply prayed, "Thy will be done" whenever I felt anxious or needed to communicate with God for peace of mind and heart. I gave up control (as if I'd ever had it!), but I consciously made the decision to give it over to God and let Him decide Jerry's fate … and mine.

Radiation Continues

We are all aware that chemotherapy is hard on a cancer patient, but radiation isn't an easy treatment option either. Jerry lost a section of his hair where he received his radiation treatments. It was there one night and gone the next morning. When I noticed the bald spot, I went looking for the lost hair and found it in the bathtub where he'd taken his shower a little earlier that morning. When I told him, as gently as I could, that his hair was falling out, he cried. It wasn't a cry that he tried to hold back. It was instant, and it broke my heart to once again be the bearer of bad news. Jerry was a proud man and having his hair fall out in a perfect circle was embarrassing for him. He tried to have his hair cut to mask the bald spot, but it only seemed to make it more obvious. Radiation was hard on his body and his emotions. Jerry spoke frequently about feeling that he was losing control of his own life.

During Jerry's hospitalization at F. F. Thompson, he began to complain of pain in his back. He'd have me rub it and try to "work it out," but I knew that it wasn't going to be that easy to get rid of it. My general experience in life told me that you never wanted to hear that a cancer patient was having back pain. It was almost always an indication that the cancer had spread to the spine. An MRI proved this. Jerry had tumors all throughout his spine. One was exceptionally large, and the doctor told us that it could cause paralysis if it didn't respond positively to radiation. While Jerry was being tattooed for his next round of radiation, Dr. B. took me privately into his office to show me the MRI results on his computer screen. I'll never forget him pointing out the tumors, of varying sizes, between *every single vertebrae* of Jerry's spine. The doctor told me to make a fist with my hand and then said, "That tumor right there," pointing to a large mass on the photo, "that one is the size of your fist. If it gets any bigger your husband will be paralyzed." He went on, like so many other medical professionals before him, to ask me if I understood the seriousness of Jerry's condition.

I responded to him in the same way that I had a dozen times before: "I know that Jerry is dying, but he's alive today, and we have to do what we can for him today." The day after Jerry ended radiation on his skull, he began radiation on his spine. He didn't get a single day's break between treatments.

Going Back to Work

By now, it was time for me to go back to work. Many people had offered to help us by driving Jerry to radiation treatments and doctor's appointments so I could get into school and prepare for the 2010–2011 school year. Jerry was very ready to spend less time with me. Some days we brought out the worst in each other. If I couldn't hide my stress and anxiety on a particular day, it made Jerry turn inward. My constant questions drove him crazy: "What's your pain level, Jerry?" "Are you hungry, Jerry?" "Did you mark your pills on the chart, Jerry?" It was time for at least one of us to get back to work and have some normalcy and sense of routine. Jerry hadn't worked since the day of his first MRI back on July 16. He missed his job as a machine equipment operator for the Village of Seneca Falls. He missed the friends that he worked with, and he missed being able to drive. Soon, I knew, he would miss deer hunting, an activity that he adored. Life was never going to be the same, and that was a painful realization.

For me, returning to work was extremely difficult. I loved having a routine and a purpose, but my mind was constantly on Jerry, and I was always worried about his pain level. I would call and text him throughout the day asking him to rate his pain from one to ten. He'd fib and tell me that he felt great and that he was enjoying the company of all of the wonderful people who checked in on him daily. There was Chuck, Paul, George, and Bob, my mother, his father, and more. Jerry had a lot of earthly angels taking care of him when I couldn't. If it hadn't been for the number of people who took it upon themselves to look after Jerry during the day, I wouldn't have been able to work as long as I did. My school administrators were very understanding and told me that I could go out on a family sick leave of absence whenever I needed to. I held off as long as I could, and Jerry held me off as long as he could. The simple truth was that Jerry's days were very difficult and painful, but he tried to hide it from me. He wanted to protect me from it for the few hours of the day that I was at work.

Hiding the Pain

One day, I left school at lunch to run to the bank before I went home to check on Jerry. Paul C. pulled up next to me in the bank parking lot looking concerned. "Nancy, Jerry is going to kill me for telling you this, but when I was out for my walk this morning, I was down the street from your house, and I could hear Jerry screaming. I ran down to your house and walked in and found Jerry trying to roll over on the couch. He's in a lot more pain than he's telling you, Nancy." I went home and demanded that Jerry let me start my leave of absence the next day, but, as usual, he overruled me. He promised me that he'd tell me when he wanted and needed me to be home full-time. Later that afternoon Jerry called Paul and yelled at him for telling me about the episode. The next morning, Paul stopped at our house to check on Jerry during his walk, just like he did every other day, and the two of them made up. I don't think they even discussed the matter. Jerry couldn't stay mad at Paul, who was a wonderful friend.

Side Effects

When Jerry began radiation on his spine, we had to accept a new side effect. When radiating his spine, the radiation went through to his esophagus. Jerry's esophagus was burned, and it was very painful to eat or drink. There was medication to numb the pain, but when Jerry would take the medicine, it would make him feel as though he wasn't able to breathe, and he'd have anxiety attacks. Nothing was ever easy. The very thing that was supposed to prolong Jerry's life was destroying the quality of what little life he had left.

Roswell Park Cancer Institute

We had waited all summer to get an appointment at Roswell Park Cancer Institute in Buffalo. Jerry and I saw the appointment at Roswell as the beginning of *real* treatment. At Roswell, they treated cancer with strong drugs like Interleukin 2 and Interferon. Jerry's oncologist had given us sincere hope that these were two options that would be presented to Jerry at Roswell. We'd been warned that either one would require an extended stay at this hospital and could bring Jerry very close to death, but it was a risk we were willing to take. Sadly, we were desperate enough to be looking forward to this form of treatment. We had a kind of "game plan" for the time that Jerry would be a patient at Roswell. I would stay in Buffalo with Jerry during the beginning and most dangerous stages of the treatment. My sister would move into our house and would be a surrogate mother to our sons. When Jerry was well enough, I'd go back to work, be with our sons during the week, and would spend the weekends in Buffalo taking care of Jerry while Joan, again, took care of the boys.

All of our eggs were in the Roswell basket, but Roswell was a complete bust. The doctors there explained to us that Interleukin 2 and Interferon would cause swelling of the spine, and because Jerry had tumors all throughout his spine, they couldn't risk paralyzing him in an attempt to cure him. They flatly turned us away. We both sat in the examining room sobbing. We walked away from Roswell totally defeated.

The Ribbon Is Black
for a Reason

It was during that visit to Roswell that I discovered the color associated with melanoma. As we all know, the breast cancer ribbon is pink. You may not have known that the color that represents leukemia is orange, and lung cancer's color is pearl. *The color that represents melanoma is black.* A family friend, Mary Ellen, had graciously offered to meet us at Roswell that day to help us navigate our way around the hospital, because she had been successfully treated for breast cancer at Roswell. She was with me in the gift shop as I was searching through a basket of wrist bands to wear in support of the different types of cancer. When I came across one for melanoma, it took my breath away. "There's a reason why the color for melanoma is black," I said. I didn't need to say anymore. Mary Ellen just looked at me sadly.

A New Egg, a New Basket

By this time, Jerry's oncologist was trying to find a clinical study for him to participate in so that he could receive a new drug referred to as PLX 4032. It was a drug that was being studied particularly in melanoma patients, and it was showing some real promise. Some melanoma patients' tumors shrunk with the use of this medication, and they lived an average of nine months longer with the drug than without it. Jerry saw this as a tremendous opportunity. Unfortunately, to be honest, I didn't, but I never told him of my concerns. Of course I wanted Jerry to live longer, but at what expense to him and our children? Was it fair to extend Jerry's life if it wasn't going to be a good life? What about when the medicine stopped working, as it was guaranteed to do? Would we just go back to this dismal life? Jerry didn't seem capable of thinking that far into the future, but I was, and the thought of it made me painfully melancholy and anxious.

PLX 4032

I had done everything possible to get Jerry to as many of our sons' soccer games as possible that fall. If memory serves me well, by the end of the season he'd only missed three or four games. The last game was Danny's sectional game; he was the team captain. Jerry missed it by only one day; he died the day before.

Jerry was particularly upset about missing a game that was played on a field that would have required him to walk up about two dozen steep steps to get to it. Jerry had had an especially grueling treatment that day along with some tests, and I knew that he wasn't physically up to walking that number of steps. I felt terrible telling Jerry no, but I knew it was for the best. When I arrived home, I found Bob G. sitting with Jerry at our dining room table. Bob is a pharmaceutical researcher for cancer drugs. Bob had heard about Jerry being interested in PLX 4032 and had called Jerry while I was at the game and offered to come over and explain how the drug worked. I'm so glad that Jerry didn't attend that game, because Bob was able to spend time with Jerry that evening demystifying the drug. He gave us both some much needed hope and solid information.

Community Support

"When I was a boy and I would see scary things in the news, my mother would say to me, 'Look for the helpers. You will always find people who are helping.' To this day, especially in times of disaster, I remember my mother's words, and I am always comforted by realizing that there are still so many helpers—so many caring people in this world."—Fred Rogers

During Jerry's illness, our community rallied. Jerry was a fixture in Seneca Falls. Everyone knew him, because of the nature of his job but also because he had coached and coordinated the youth lacrosse program for many years. Because of Jerry's kind nature, people truly felt connected to him. The first large scale proof of that connection, love, and support was when the Seneca Falls Police Department arranged a chili cook-off in Jerry's honor. The soccer program piggybacked on that opportunity and sold baked goods and chances to win gift baskets that were donated by many generous people who wanted to do something to help us. The chili cook-off was an enormous success.

Several groups of friends and families merged as teams and tried to out-cook each other in order to win the First Annual SFPD Chili Cook-Off. A local blues band played upbeat music while people mingled, drank a little, ate a lot, and enjoyed the day tremendously. Many of Jerry's old high school friends attended, giving the class of 1982 a chance to have a mini class reunion. I couldn't begin to guess how many people attended that event. There were even people who introduced themselves that day, shyly admitting that they were strangers who had just heard about the man from Seneca Falls who had cancer and that they wanted to come out to support us. Our local senator also attended the cook-off. Most importantly, our family and friends were there, showing all of the love that they'd been showing since the day we first heard the word "cancer." The money raised was intended to help cover traveling expenses from treatments, which now spanned a much larger region than Canandaigua, Buffalo, and Rochester.

Decisions ... Decisions

Behind the scenes, I was under tremendous stress. Important decisions had to be made, and I was the only one who could make them. Jerry had two very different opportunities. One was to go to The Cancer Treatment Centers of America in Philadelphia, Pennsylvania and the other was to go to Vanderbilt University in Nashville, Tennessee to participate in a clinical trial. Jerry had been turned down for other clinical trials due to the tumors in his spine. The people from The Cancer Treatment Centers of America were wonderful to us on the phone. They agreed to arrange and pay for our airline tickets and most of our expenses in Philadelphia. In Tennessee, we would be on our own financially, but all of our doctors agreed that Jerry's real hope lay in that drug. Really, it wasn't a difficult decision to make after all. We *had* to go to Tennessee.

Vanderbilt University
Nashville, Tennessee

The day after the chili cook-off, Vanderbilt University's Cancer Center contacted Jerry and asked us to be in Tennessee the following day! With absolutely no time to lose, I booked flights, found a hotel, and, fortunately, my brother offered to fly to Tennessee with us to help me transport Jerry. At that point, Jerry was unable to walk through an airport to get from one gate to the next. He needed a wheelchair and assistance from an airport employee. The first indication of how difficult traveling was going to be happened while going through security. An airline assistant took Jerry to the security area for people in wheelchairs while Mike and I went through the normal security procedures. Although we were literally just a few feet away from Jerry, I could see him crying. His anxiety had been getting the best of him, and this situation was way more than he could take. When we had all gone through security successfully, we sat for quite a while before boarding our flight. Jerry sat with Mike and had a cup of coffee. I fed him one pill after another. There were pills for pain and pills for anxiety. I think, in truth, I overmedicated him on that first flight, because he got very loopy and fell asleep shortly after we boarded. If I hadn't had Mike to help me on that trip to Tennessee, it would have been sheer hell. I know that for a fact, because Mike had to return home before Jerry and I did, so I brought Jerry home by myself. It was worse than hell.

When we arrived at our hotel in Nashville we had to wait about two hours before our room was ready. Mike tried to keep Jerry's mind busy. They took a very short walk outside to see the football stadium at Vanderbilt University. We sat in the hotel lounge very tired, each thinking private thoughts. Finally, our rooms were cleaned and we moved into them and got settled.

Jerry went to sleep almost immediately, and I used my laptop to get on Facebook to let our friends and family know that we had arrived safely. The next day, Jerry and I were to meet with the doctor in charge of the clinical study at Vanderbilt at 3:40 p.m. Mike would fly out early that morning, so I was on my own with a very sick husband, and I was scared. Nashville, Tennessee is a large city, and I didn't dare wander too far, but Mike texted me later in the afternoon of the day we arrived to let me know that he was downstairs at the bar having a beer. I texted back, "Stay put. I'm on my way down." I left Jerry a note (he was still asleep) telling him where we were and left instructions to call or text as soon as he woke up.

Although that time with my brother was brief, it did me a lot of good. Mike and I spoke honestly about everything that had happened from my point of view. I clearly remember telling him, "I know that I'll never bring Jerry back to Tennessee no matter what that doctor says tomorrow. Jerry's going to die before we ever get a chance to come back here." The truth is there had been a dark change in Jerry. I felt as though, when I looked into Jerry's eyes, I could see right through him. It was as if his body was here but his spirit was no longer with us. Later, I read a book by author Mark Matousek called *Sex Death Enlightenment*. In that book, Mr. Matousek speaks openly about all of the friends he's lost to AIDS. He described what I saw in Jerry perfectly when he said, "The dying have eyes on both sides of their heads, feet pointing in two directions." It's so true. It's as if the dying person is halfway in the physical world and halfway in the spiritual world.

Mike said that he was glad that we'd had that conversation; that he had been concerned that I was putting a lot of faith in this treatment. I assured him that I wasn't. I knew better. The writing was on the wall. I was able to be honest with my brother as he offered a kind and nonjudgmental ear.

I sent regular text messages to Jerry's cell phone while Mike and I were downstairs in the hotel, but he didn't respond, so we assumed that he was still asleep. My messages were always the same: Mike and I are right downstairs, next to the lounge, at the bar, and all he had to do was text or call me when he woke up, and we'd be there in seconds. Finally, I received a text which simply said, "HELP." With my heart pounding, I ran into our hotel room to find Jerry crying and shaking. Apparently, when he woke up, he had struggled to use his keyboard to text me and he couldn't remember how to call me. He finally managed to peck out the letters H-E-L-P. The short time that I had spent with my brother left me with tremendous guilt, but I was able to settle Jerry down fairly quickly. I gave him his medicine and we took him out for a fabulous steak dinner that night.

Because Jerry was able to walk short distances, we found a steak house that wasn't far from the hotel. One of the odd things about Jerry's cancer is that it didn't emaciate him. He didn't look skinny and stricken like other very sick cancer patients. Due to the dosage of steroids that Jerry was taking, he looked puffy and more overweight than he actually was. His appetite was ravenous. Mike and Jerry ordered delicious steak dinners, and I watched my husband enjoy every bite of that meal with his beloved brother-in-law. Part of me was so grateful to see him enjoy his food, but when I looked at Jerry, I couldn't help but see the death in his eyes. It just confirmed my belief that Jerry's time was very short.

The next morning when we woke up, Mike was already gone. He texted me during his layover in Charlotte, North Carolina and asked if I was holding up okay. Jerry slept most of the day. He needed to be as strong and rested as possible during his exam at Vanderbilt. As he put it, he had to be Superman and show the doctors that he could do whatever was necessary in order to be considered a candidate for this clinical study. To this very day, I don't know how Jerry did the things that he did during that exam. He was able to lift his arms above his head, touch his toes and walk a short distance unassisted. Physically, these things shouldn't have been possible. After a lengthy exam, the doctor told us that Jerry was a good candidate for one of the clinical trials. We would have to go home and sit out a "washout" period of his last radiation treatments, which had targeted a large tumor in his shoulder, and then we could return the week of November 8, just two weeks away. We cried with relief and joy when they told us that Jerry could receive this medication. Some people's tumors shrunk 100 percent for up to nine months while on the drug. I tried not to think about what would happen after the nine-month period, because, in truth, I already knew … the tumors would begin to grow again, and then we'd be back to square one. But if Jerry could get relief from his cancer for up to nine months and see our son, Danny, graduate from high school in June, that would be a huge blessing.

The details of the clinical trial were overwhelming at best. The plan went something like this: Jerry and I would fly to Tennessee in two weeks and stay for about five days while he underwent several tests. The doctors would administer the medication. Then, we'd fly home only to fly back again two weeks later. The trips every two weeks would last for a while, and then the time in between trips to Tennessee would extend to four weeks and then more. The doctor said that at some point they'd try to move us into a similar study in New York City to ease the burden of all of the traveling. Later, as the winter progressed into one of the worst winters we'd had in years, I'd think about what it would have been like traveling with a sick husband every two to four weeks to Tennessee for treatments. I admit that it would have been a very difficult routine to adjust to. Although my sister was on deck to take care of our sons every time we had to go to Tennessee, the emotional, financial, and personal strain of a routine like this would have done its damage.

Changes

"I'm sick and tired of being sick
and tired."—Jerry Galusha

Sadly, I saw Jerry literally deflate the minute we got back to the hotel that day. The pain in his shoulder, which had been briefly alleviated from radiation, came back with a vengeance. I dreaded the trip home to Seneca Falls the next day, but it was my responsibility to take the best care of Jerry that I could, and I can honestly say that it was an honor and a privilege. It never mattered how exhausted I was. I knew that Jerry's time was limited, and I wanted him to leave this Earth knowing that I'd loved him and cared for him in ways that I'd never had to before and that I would have done it for as long as necessary.

On the plane home, Jerry's pain became outrageous. I applied more pain patches on his arm than I had a right to. I knew that we were using too much pain medication than was really safe, but my goal was to get him home before he became completely unglued. He was very testy as well—borderline mean. But I knew that it was because of his pain, so I tried to ignore it without letting it hurt my feelings. My sister-in-law, Mary, picked us up at the airport in Syracuse. By this time, Jerry couldn't even be reasonable. He was very demanding that evening. At one point, he got so mad at me that he wheeled himself away, turned his back on me, and stared out of the door of the airport. I literally felt forsaken. The person who needed me the most couldn't even look at me.

Our drive home was terrible. Jerry continuously told Mary to slow down as he moaned and groaned in pain. These were behaviors that I was getting used to while taking care of Jerry, but no one else had seen them. I was embarrassed to have Mary witness Jerry's behavior and tried to just keep talking in order to minimize what Mary would see and hear. I'm sure it didn't work.

When we arrived home an hour later, the boys were thrilled to see us, but Jerry had changed drastically during that trip. He wasn't the same person, and it only continued to get worse. Jerry's shoulder pain was unbearable. The dosage of several of his medications increased, and doctors prescribed new medication the following week, but nothing helped.

God, What's Taking You So Long?

Jerry hadn't slept in our bed very often since his diagnosis. Our bed simply wasn't comfortable for him once the tumors in his spine and hips became more prominent. But one night, shortly after we came home from Tennessee, Jerry announced, "I'm sleeping in bed tonight. I'm exhausted and need to stretch out." I was happy for the company but wondered if he'd sleep well. As soon as we lay down I realized how labored Jerry's breathing was. His breaths seemed to come few and far between. I knew that narcotics slowed down his respiratory system, but, still, it made me very nervous to lie beside Jerry and wait for his next breath to eventually come. I also realized how close to death we were now. *One of these days*, I thought, *he's just going to stop breathing.* Fear overtook me that night. It was paralyzing to lie next to Jerry counting the seconds between his breaths. I tried to calm myself by praying from deep within my heart, "God, what's taking you so long? Hasn't he suffered enough? Surely there's room for

Jerry in heaven. If you love him, why won't you just take him?"

Lying there, I made a pact with myself, because I honestly believed that Jerry might die that night. If Jerry stopped breathing, I would allow him to stay there in bed, peacefully, and in the morning, after the boys went to school, I'd call the mortician. I would not call 911. I would not try to resuscitate him. I would allow God to take my Jerry, to put him out of his suffering. I loved Jerry enough to let him go.

At about 11:30 p.m. Jerry woke up with a start and ran straight to the bathroom. I was sure that he was going to vomit but instead he moaned loudly. Then I heard him move quickly to the kitchen and gulp down pills with water, and before I knew it, he ran back to the bedroom and quite literally jumped into bed. You wonder why I didn't get up and assist him? First of all, he did this all so quickly that he was back in bed before I had woken up enough to take in the feat that he'd just performed. I sincerely didn't have time to wake up enough to chase him. Secondly, he scared me. I didn't know what was happening, and I don't think I really wanted to find out. That's the honest truth. I was afraid. It's not what I want to admit, but it's true.

When Jerry jumped back into bed, I wondered how he had physically accomplished it. He shouldn't have been able to run. He should have been screaming in pain. When he got back into bed, Jerry shook so hard the entire bed vibrated. During those next moments, I realized that Jerry was hallucinating. He moaned and groaned and babbled on about putting his body parts on the black and white lines, one part at a time, until the pain decreased, and then he'd move onto the next body part. He listed all of the bones and organs that hurt, placing them mentally on the black line until the line turned white and the pain was under control. Witnessing this experience was terrifying. When he settled down, I couldn't help myself and said, "Jerry, what the hell just happened?" He mumbled something about getting his pain under control and fell back to sleep. The next morning, Jerry apologized. He said that he couldn't explain why he did what he did other than to say that it was the only way he could handle the pain, to deal with each painful bone and organ, one at a time, until the pills had kicked in and he could fall back to sleep. Those black and white lines appeared again later in the week.

The Beginning of the End

On the Saturday after our trip to Tennessee, I woke up to the sound of Jerry vomiting violently. He had gotten up earlier and took one of every pill he had. He wasn't trying to harm himself. He was desperate to get out of the pain that was crushing him. His greatest fear was being readmitted to the hospital and undergoing more radiation.

In order to participate in the clinical trial at Vanderbilt, he couldn't have any more radiation. He really didn't need to worry, because, in truth, radiation was no longer an option. He'd had three rounds of it, back to back, and the radiologist and oncologist said that his body could not handle any more for at least eighteen months. The cancer had done nothing but grow during his radiation and chemotherapy treatments. He had been taking chemotherapy in pills (Temodar) that made him vomit every morning, and it hadn't done one bit of good. A PET scan the week before we went to Tennessee confirmed that he now had cancer on his liver, lungs, and adrenal glands. And most of the tumors that had been there earlier were now even larger. All of this pain and suffering, all of these pills, all of this radiation had been for nothing … Jerry's cancer was like a monster taking over his whole body. It was destroying Jerry, the person I loved.

I tried to negotiate with Jerry that Saturday morning. I told him that if he would let me take him to the hospital, they might be able to get his pain under control enough for us to go back to Vanderbilt and start the clinical trial on time. In this kind of pain, I'd never be able to get him on a plane. I also told him that if I had to call an ambulance, it would upset the boys and our neighbors. Basically, I wanted to get him out of the house and into the hospital with as little fanfare as possible. An hour later, he finally agreed to go, warning me, "I'm going to say some awful things on our way there. You're going to have to forgive me." He made good on that promise. I got him to F. F. Thompson's emergency room within forty minutes. We were the only people in the ER, and they took Jerry into a room very quickly when they recognized the severity of his condition. The ER doctor was a good man. I liked him immediately. He was no nonsense and told Jerry that the likelihood of him going back to Tennessee had diminished tremendously. Jerry seemed to hear and comprehend very little of what the doctor said, but I was selfishly relieved that for once, a medical professional was giving Jerry bad news instead of me.

The doctor administered a very strong pain medication, Dilaudid, through his IV every five minutes, but even then, his pain was off the charts. At one point, to ease Jerry's anxiety, I ran my hand over his head and felt a new lump. I instantly became nauseous. I knew that this was another metastases. A test earlier in the week confirmed that his brain was clear of cancer, but this was another one on his skull. God, another skull-based tumor? How long would it be before his cancer found its way inside his skull and into his brain? From my reading, I knew that many melanoma patients are ultimately diagnosed because the cancer had made its way into the brain. I understood that it was just a matter of time. The ER doctor confirmed that this was likely another metastases, but I never told Jerry. He didn't need to know.

The ER doctor took me aside a while later, when Jerry was finally getting a little pain relief, and asked me if I had considered Jerry's end of life care yet. I wasn't shocked by his question. I had expected this conversation to take place eventually. The doctor asked if I'd signed a DNR (do not resuscitate order), and I told him that I hadn't but that I was now prepared to. Watching my husband's life go completely to hell was agonizing, and my conscience would not allow me to do anything to prolong his suffering. We didn't need Jerry to actually sign the DNR, but the doctor felt that we did need him to verbally agree to it. He helped me broach the subject with Jerry. He was honest and got right to the point, explaining that if Jerry's body decided that it had had enough, he might be able to be resuscitated, but it would come at a cost. Pounding on his chest and using machines to force Jerry not to die was the only option, and Jerry said that he didn't want that to happen. But in the very next breath, he said, "But I still want to go to Tennessee next week." I don't believe that Jerry understood that we expected his death to come so soon. I think that he tried to believe that we were making reference to sometime down the road—if the medicine in Tennessee didn't work.

I slipped into an unoccupied room to call my sons, who were home together awaiting news of their father's current condition. Danny answered the phone and I explained, as calmly as I could, that Dad was in very serious condition now and that he likely had days to weeks to live. I couldn't lie to the boys. I had promised them from the very beginning that I'd be honest, even if the truth was painful. Danny asked many questions, mostly about how his father was taking the news. "Is Dad okay with this, Mom?" he asked more than once. Danny needed to talk to his father and get a feel for whether or not his dad was accepting his death. I tried to reassure him that his father understood that his life was coming to an end soon.

Danny passed the phone to Phillip. I told him the same thing that I had told Danny. I could hear little sobs, but Phillip had been a rock through Jerry's illness. He rarely cried, and that scared me. Phillip and Danny chose to be alone that afternoon. I offered to send my mother, brother or sister, or all three of them over to our house, but the boys made a pact to be together and help each other digest the fact that they would lose their beloved father very soon. Later in the day, Phillip went to a friend's house and Danny went to my mother's, as she had offered to cook him dinner. Danny never ate that evening. He entered my mother's house, collapsed into my sister's arms, and allowed her to comfort him until he fell deeply into sleep. It was probably the best sleep he'd had in weeks.

The next day, I took both of the boys to F. F. Thompson Hospital to visit their father. Phillip didn't stay in his dad's room long. I believe that he'd privately said good-bye to his dad much earlier in his illness and that a formal good-bye wasn't necessary or tolerable. There really wasn't much he had left to say, and watching his father struggle to make sense or speak in complete sentences had become more painful than the thought of losing him. Danny asked for private time with his father before we left. I stood by the door to monitor the situation. I was trying to balance what I thought Danny needed with what I thought Danny should have to take in. Although it probably wasn't the "right" thing to do, I listened in to make sure that nothing was said that could cause Danny any more grief than he was already experiencing. I overhead Jerry tell Danny that he was afraid that I'd given up on the idea of taking him to Tennessee and encouraged Danny to talk to me about it. They dropped an F-bomb or two during this honest conversation, and, although I bristled at the sound of the word which we never allowed ourselves to speak at home, I had to let that go. They needed to be frank and open and honest, and if that included some swearing, it was acceptable at this time. What they said was true: "This f——ing sucked!"

I made arrangements to miss the first couple of days of work that week to see where things stood, but I made it clear that I would probably begin taking my family leave of absence. After the first full day of the new week, I realized, undoubtedly, that Jerry needed me to advocate for him full-time. I needed to be Jerry's voice and his reasoning, because the levels of his medication, which now included methadone, made it impossible for him to stay with a clear thought or speak coherently for more than a minute or two at a time.

Friends started to appear at the hospital. They all

knew that they were coming to say a final good-bye It was agonizing to watch, because Jerry had wonderful friends who loved him dearly. I wouldn't have taken that time away from them for anything, though. I felt free to leave and go home to the boys when Jerry had evening visitors. It was hard to be *his* wife and *their* mother at this time. I didn't know how or when to split my roles. Jerry's father also spent many hours with him each day, and Jerry's brother had made the trip from Virginia to New York to be with him during his last days.

When Times Get Tough, Eat Ziti

"We are only as strong as we are united, as
weak as we are divided."—J. K. Rowling,
Harry Potter and the Goblet of Fire

The second fundraiser to benefit our family was held on November 2, and was hosted by the Mynderse Academy Boys and Girls Soccer Club, It was a ziti dinner. Our primarily Italian small town often held ziti dinners to raise money for organizations or families in need. I called my friend Chris, who was involved with this project, the morning of the dinner to ask her for an approximate number of people that I'd be facing that night. You see, I wasn't used to attending public events without Jerry, and I was nervous. Chris told me that they'd sold about two hundred tickets, and I felt that I could handle that number of people without too much emotion. When I arrived later that day, I couldn't find a free parking space in the parking lot, down the entire street, or even on the little side streets around the club where the dinner was held. Hundreds of people came out to support my family;

most of them had not bought a ticket in advance. The wonderful volunteers who planned the dinner had cooked for about four hundred people, but even that number was a low approximation. In the end, the organizers had to turn people away, because they just couldn't make the food stretch any further.

I was about twenty minutes late to the dinner, because I had stayed at the hospital longer than I had anticipated that afternoon to make arrangements for Jerry to be transferred on Thursday to The House of John, a hospice house, where Jerry could die as peacefully as possible in a less institutional setting than the hospital. Jerry had agreed to these arrangements. On Monday, the day before the dinner, the doctors had told him that he had about three months to live. He took the news very hard, but, because of all the medication he was taking, he didn't really concentrate on his prognosis for long periods of time. I was usually able to distract his thoughts when he brought it up.

When I found a parking spot that afternoon, created only because someone had pulled out at the perfect time, I stepped out onto the parking lot and burst into tears, feeling completely overwhelmed. A friend spotted me and came to hug me and encourage me until I gathered my wits and was able to walk into the SMS (Societa DiMuto Soccorso) Italian Club. Relief washed over me when I saw, sitting at the nearest table, my friends from Romulus Central School, the school that I had left only a year before.

Family photo taken the night of Danny's homecoming dance, one month before Jerry's death.

One of Jerry's favorite activities was to hunt deer.

Nancy, Danny (middle), and Phillip two years after Jerry's death.

Helmet presented to Nancy at the playground
dedication in honor of Jerry. This helmet is currently on
display at the Seneca Falls Community Center.

Nancy, Danny, and Phillip hugging each other at the playground dedication as Jerry's father and brother look on.

The sign at the entrance of the Jerry Galusha Memorial Playground.

The Galusha, Midey, Blanchard, Fera, Dreitlein, and Manzari families at the playground dedication.

Jerry's sons, Danny and Phillip, the night of Danny's graduation from high school.

I had worked there as an elementary school teacher for twenty-two years when I left to take the job at Seneca Falls Middle School as a librarian. My friends hadn't forgotten me and were all there to support me. Among so many family members, friends, acquaintances, and total strangers, I felt entirely loved. While hundreds of people ate, others came and took their food home, because there was nowhere left to sit. The organizers conducted several raffles, and squeals of "I won!" could be heard all over the club. It was so festive that for a few moments, I was actually able to forget why I was there. Although I had expected him, Jerry's father never arrived at the club that evening, as he had decided to stay with his dying son and forego the dinner. I'm sure that he never regretted his decision. Any time spent with Jerry at that point was cherished time.

It was at that event that a friend from Romulus Central School took me aside and very seriously asked me, "Nancy, how are you holding up? I mean, I look at you, and you would have every right to be falling apart, to be in a million pieces. How are you not falling apart?" I looked Joe in the eyes and stated the facts: "Joe, look around. Look at my support. How can I fall down when I have an entire community holding me and my family up? They won't let me fall apart."

Exhausted that night, I answered the phone at about 8:15 p.m. to a familiar voice. It was one of Jerry's close elderly relatives. She had gotten the news of our plans to transfer Jerry from the hospital to the hospice house on Thursday, and she was not happy about that decision. She felt that I was giving up hope and wanted me to try to bring Jerry home instead of to hospice. She was desperate to find a way to convince me that Jerry's condition was not as serious as I said it was. I understood that she spoke to me out of pure love, but, still, it hurt to have my decisions and motives questioned. This person, whom my husband loved dearly, had been married more than twice the number of years that I had been. However, she had never had to sit at her husband's death bed, making the heartrending decisions that I was being forced to make. I would never wish my circumstances on anyone, but, as I explained to her, whenever I had to make a particularly difficult decision for Jerry, I'd ask myself just one question: "What would I want Jerry to do for me if I were in his shoes?" I let that simple question guide all of my difficult decisions. If I could look myself in the mirror when I answered it, I knew that I had made the right choice. It took some patient explaining, but she eventually accepted my decision. It just took her a little more time to digest the fact that we were going to lose Jerry very soon.

More White and Black Lines

At 10:15 that night, the phone rang again. I slept with the phone on my bed, as Jerry didn't always understand the time of day and would, on occasion, want to hear my voice at odd hours.

"Hi Jerry, what's up? Are you okay?" I asked.

"Nancy, do you remember Dr. Henry from the summer?" Henry was one of the doctors that we'd met during Jerry's previous stay at F. F. Thompson Hospital a couple of months earlier. Jerry liked Henry and trusted him.

"Yes, Jerry. I remember Henry. Why?"

"Well, Dr. Henry told me that if we line my medicine up just right, on the white line, I might still be able to go to Tennessee." Jerry had been talking about white lines and black lines for about a week. To this day, I really don't understand where those lines came from, but I accept that it's a question that'll never be answered.

My heart sank into my stomach; a feeling that I was almost used to by now.

"Jerry, is Dr. Henry there with you now? Put him on the phone if he is."

"Hello, Mrs. Galusha," Henry said, politely. He spoke to me as he stepped out into the hall so we could have a private conversation without upsetting or offending Jerry. "Henry, please tell me that you didn't tell Jerry that I could take him to Tennessee, because if you did, I'll be furious with you!"

"Mrs. Galusha, I just heard everything that your husband said. I can see very clearly that Jerry's condition has deteriorated tremendously since we met last summer. I heard everything that he told you, and I want to assure you that I said about half of what he told you just now." Henry admitted that he didn't think that Jerry, personally, was ready for hospice, because he was still counting on going to Tennessee. I explained to Henry that the clinical trial in Tennessee was no longer an option and that I had made up my mind about taking Jerry to The House of John. I sincerely wanted Jerry to die in a more tranquil setting than the hospital. Henry asked me about Jerry's white and black lines. I obviously couldn't enlighten him.

I told Henry that he had to be firm but kind to Jerry. I asked him not to give Jerry any false hope about going to Tennessee, because Jerry was blaming me for preventing it. When Jerry got back on the phone, I told him not to worry about Tennessee, that I would absolutely take him at a later date, when we got his pain under control. I hope that Jerry slept a little more peacefully that night after I reassured him that his spot on the clinical trial list was still open to him.

The Next Morning

"Jordy, may I ask you something?" I approached Jerry's nurse the next morning. Jordy was an amazing nurse. She was tough as nails and didn't sugarcoat anything, which made her exactly the type of person that I needed during these last days with Jerry.

"What is it, honey?"

"Jordy, Jerry's dying, right? I mean, I'm not jumping to conclusions or fast-forwarding things in my mind, am I?"

"Oh, Nancy, honey, no, you're not jumping to conclusions. Jerry is dying."

"How long, Jordy? I mean, is it still days or weeks?"

"I can't say for sure, but I know that he doesn't have weeks to live. Hours to days, honey. What's going on? Why are you asking? I thought you understood."

I regurgitated the details of the conversation with the relative who had called the night before; the one who had made me question myself and my understanding of where exactly Jerry stood in the short timeline of his life.

It seemed to me that Jerry was dangling between life and death, and death was winning.

Friends continued to come to say good-bye. I welcomed them because I knew that they needed to see Jerry one last time. Their love and concern was sincere, and I took great comfort in the fact that Jerry was on the receiving end of all of this love. That day was Wednesday and Melissa, Jerry's dear friend from high school, visited one last time. She brought him fried chicken for lunch. Jerry made little sense that morning and early afternoon. But one thing was clear; Jerry did not want to say good-bye to Melissa. When he understood that Melissa was leaving, he grasped onto her and begged her not to go. He cried into her loving arms, and my heart broke for her. I could tell that she wanted to stay for him but needed to leave to get to work. Eventually, Melissa backed away, tears in her eyes, shaking her head. What had happened to the Jerry Galusha she had known? This certainly wasn't the same person.

Jerry ate a piece of fried chicken that afternoon with his eyes closed. Clearly, he was hungry, but sleep overtook him. I put the remainder of the food in the garbage can sensing that it was the last time that he'd eat. I was right.

Early Morning Phone Calls
Are Never Good News

At 6:30 the next morning, the phone rang at home. At that hour of the day, it's never a good sign. A nurse explained that Jerry had taken a turn for the worse in the night, going into respiratory failure. Some measures had been taken and he'd pulled through, even though he clearly had a DNR bracelet on his wrist. Frantically, I woke the boys up and told them that if they wanted to see their dad, perhaps for the last time, they could come with me to the hospital, but if they chose not to come, they could either go to school or stay home; whatever they wanted to do was fine with me. The rule throughout Jerry's illness was that there were no rules. I completely left it up to them, and they both chose to go with me to the hospital that morning. My brother called as we were on our way to Canandaigua and said that he'd checked on Jerry on his way to work and that Jerry appeared to be comfortable but pretty incoherent.

The boys and I arrived at the hospital at about 7:30 a.m. Jerry's eyes were open, but it was hard to tell how much he understood. His father arrived shortly after we did. It was evident that we weren't going to be transferring Jerry to the House of John that day because, frankly, we didn't expect him to live through the day. My sister had called her children who were both attending college in nearby Rochester, and they arrived next. As I said earlier, their father had died just three and a half years before, in a car accident. Due to the nature of their father's death, they didn't get the opportunity to literally say good-bye to him, so it was important to them to spend some time with their Uncle Jerry and have closure. Unfortunately, Uncle Jerry was no longer the man that they had known. My brother, sister-in-law, and niece, Rachel, also arrived a little later. Everyone was there to say good-bye.

Phillip approached his dad. He had important news to share with his father who had always encouraged the boys to try new things.

"Dad, I made the basketball team."

Jerry looked at me, confused. I said, "Jerry, do you remember that Phillip tried out for the modified basketball team? Well, yesterday he found out that he made the team. Isn't that great?" Jerry nodded his head, but I don't know if he understood any of what we had just told him. Phillip backed out of the room with my brother. He'd seen enough. Mike took him to the cafeteria to get him some breakfast. Phillip never saw his father again.

Jerry's nieces and nephew cried at his bedside, each taking turns telling him how much they loved him. Suddenly, Jerry became angry and very anxious. He tried desperately to sit up and get out of bed. In his fit of rage he yelled, "No! No! No!" I shooed everyone out of his room. I hated the thought of the kids seeing Jerry in this state.

The anger that I saw on Jerry's face was intense. He was pissed—pissed that cancer was going to take him away from everything and everyone that he loved. He was also clearly angry that he'd been catheterized during the night without his knowledge, or undoubtedly, his consent. He reached for the tube in an attempt to try to pull it out, but I was able to stop him. A nurse bustled in and helped us calm Jerry down by administering his next dose of anxiety medication, which quickly put Jerry into a calm, peaceful state. Those three words, "No! No! No!" were the last words I ever heard my husband speak. That fact continues to haunt me today. I so wish he could have found peace with his diagnosis and prognosis, but he simply couldn't. It wasn't in his character to leave loved ones behind with so much important work left to do. The day he was told that he had only three months left to live, he frantically waved a photo of our niece Tricia in my face saying, "I can't die! I put air in her tires for her!" Jerry was a loving uncle until his very last breath.

Danny sat at his father's bedside for several hours that morning. I believe that he'd made a pact with himself that he would be there to comfort his father and to be with him when he died. Danny wouldn't eat or drink anything. I was called out into the hall by Dr. Henry to discuss Jerry's levels of medication and Danny followed me. He wanted to be involved in all decision-making, and I respected his need for that involvement. The doctor explained that although they couldn't administer lethal levels of medication, if we wanted to avoid future outbursts and anxiety, they could increase dosages to keep Jerry in a sedated state from here on in. Eventually, it would lead to respiratory failure, but Danny and I quickly agreed that this was the kindest thing that we could do for his dad. Privately, I felt that it was also the kindest thing that we could do for everyone who would come to see Jerry for the last time. Witnessing that outburst earlier was very traumatic, and I did not want Jerry to feel that level of anxiety ever again. No good could come of it.

Finally, Danny agreed to eat lunch with his grandfather. I had been trying to think of a way to give Danny the chance to leave if he needed or wanted to. I told him the truth as I saw it. I said, "You know, Dan, when Grandpa was dying, I wanted so badly to be with him, but he managed to die alone. Same with Grandma; I sat for days with her so she wouldn't die without me, but she died shortly after I left her side. Now Dad is dying, and he may not want to do it with all of us here. Sometimes, people wait for everyone to leave before they let go. If you feel comfortable with that thought, it is perfectly okay for you to leave. Dad knows that you were here, and he knows that you love him." With that, Danny made the decision to leave, and I don't have any reason to believe that he ever regretted it.

Waiting

Things quieted down for a while. All of the kids left, and Jerry's father got a ride home. He was exhausted. The impending death of his youngest son had taken a great toll on him. He looked as though he'd aged ten years in the past four months.

Just when I thought that I might be able to close my eyes for a few minutes, well-intentioned relatives began to arrive. Jerry's breathing was labored, and his lungs made horrible gurgling sounds as he attempted to take in big, gulping breaths that rocked his body. Quite frankly, Jerry looked horrible. He wouldn't have wanted to be seen or remembered that way. As Jerry's relatives gathered, his hospital room grew crowded, and I felt as if I was being squeezed out. They began to make calls to their children, telling them to come to the hospital to see Jerry before he died. I knew that there were going to be more visitors shortly, and it was making me very anxious. I began to panic; I felt that I was losing control of the situation. I've only had one full-blown anxiety attack in my life, and that was shortly after my brother-in-law died. I felt the same horrible feeling as I left the room and located two hospice nurses. I asked them to help me to empty Jerry's room in the most polite manner possible. I didn't want to offend anyone, but this was getting to be way too much for me emotionally. I needed Jerry's room to be a place of peace and quiet, his sanctuary.

The nurses asked the visitors to leave the room so they could readjust Jerry's position and make him comfortable. They all left the room but reconvened in the hall outside the door, where the chaos grew. In an attempt to calm myself down, after the nurses left, I picked up a set of handsome, wooden rosary beads that a minister had left for Jerry and tried to pray with the rosary. I hadn't used a rosary in many weeks, but Jerry had been dutifully using this one, so I could almost feel his life's energy in it as I held it. I began, "Hail Mary, full of grace." I heard more, new voices in the hall just outside the door. "Hail Mary, full of grace ...." It was no use. I couldn't concentrate. I was a mess, and I knew that what I was about to do might have been impolite or ungracious, but I calmly walked out into the hall and said, *May I ask you all a favor?*" They looked up in unison. "I should have had at least thirty more years with Jerry, and now I don't know if I'll even have thirty more minutes. I'm going to be selfish today. Could I ask you each go into his room for five minutes to say good-bye? And then I'd appreciate it if you'd allow me to be alone with Jerry for the rest of the time that he has left."

I had been so impressed with this same group of people when my mother-in-law lay dying five years before. They had devoted countless hours to being by her side, but for some reason I couldn't have them do the same for

Jerry. I wasn't comfortable with this, and I felt that I had to honor my husband's privacy, and, admittedly, I wanted his end to be between him and me.

For weeks after Jerry's death, I was consumed by guilt over my reaction to their attempted vigil and how I had interrupted it. Did I really have a right to take away their last moments with Jerry? I still don't know the answer, but at the time, it was what I felt I had to do for myself and for Jerry. Being alone with Jerry that afternoon was probably the only thing that kept me from having an anxiety attack.

A little while later, as I sat with my husband quietly meditating on the day's events I heard my brother and sister's quiet voices in the hall. They had come back to support me but didn't come back into Jerry's room as they understood that looking at Jerry and physically being present with him was truly unnecessary. I took breaks and sat with them for a few minutes at a time but would return frequently to check on Jerry. Nurses came and suctioned out his mouth as his body systems were slowly shutting down They tried to keep him comfortable and looking as normal as possible, I believe, for him and for me.

Late in the afternoon, a hospice nurse came back to ask me about my plans for the night. "Do you want a bed brought in so you can stay here tonight, or are you going to go home?" Clearly, Jerry's death was taking longer than anyone expected. Jerry's heart was strong, and he had been well-nourished and hydrated. These circumstances prolonged Jerry's life. I struggled to make a decision and then she helped me by asking, "If Jerry could speak to you right now, what do you think he'd tell you to do?" That was easy. Jerry would tell me to go home and be with our sons. I appreciated her help in making the decision. She didn't tell me what to do, but she asked the simple question that helped me make my own, correct decision.

I spent a few minutes with Jerry before I left. My brother and sister waiting to walk me outside to my van. I told him, "Jerry, obviously you're going to do this your way and in your own time. I love you so much, and I'm so sorry that our time is being cut short. I have to go home and be with the boys. If you need to leave during the night, I understand. It's okay. I'll see you again when my time here is done. I need you to look after the boys when I can't. That's a job that I'm leaving up to you. I love you, Jerry Galusha, and I've been honored to be your wife." I kissed him and left feeling completely at peace with my decision.

The Last Twenty-Four Hours

I spent a quiet evening with our sons and appreciated the time that I was being given to just be their mom. I had been very uncomfortable with amount of time that I had had to call on others to mother my sons, but I knew that we'd be spending a lot more time together very soon.

That night, I took the house phone and my cell phone into bed with me. I expected a call in the night informing me that it was over, and I was very surprised when I woke up the next morning, realizing that Jerry must have made it through the night. I hurriedly took a shower and gave the boys the option of going to school or not. I didn't know how they were functioning at school but was proud of both of them for opting to attend school that day. I think that they received a lot of support from friends, teachers, administrators, and the school counselor and that it really was the best place for them during these difficult days.

On my way to the hospital, I passed a white SUV. Looking at the driver, I realized that it was my friend, Laura, who had buried her young husband six years before. She was driving to work as I was driving to the hospital in the same situation that she had been in just a few years ago. The look on her face when she recognized me made me cry. I could tell that her heart was breaking for me. She felt so badly that I was walking the same path that she had. Although our husbands' illnesses had been different, the outcome was going to be the same, and she knew that it would get worse before it got better.

I entered Jerry's hospital room that morning. He was much quieter than he had been the day before. His breathing was steady and slow. He looked more peaceful. I wished that his relatives could have seen him like this instead of the sight that he had been the day before. I would have let them stay and sit with him longer if he'd looked this peaceful. A wave of guilt washed over me as I remembered asking them all to leave. It had truly been his dignity that I was trying to protect. I sat all that day with Jerry. The only visitors that I had were my devoted brother and sister who came to take me out to lunch. I felt comfortable leaving with them only because nothing was changing. Jerry's breathing neither slowed down nor sped up. It was as if he could go on like this for a very long time, and I think that I tried to convince myself that Jerry would make it through the weekend.

It was during these hours of sitting alone at my husband's bedside that I wrote his obituary. I wanted to honor him in the best way possible. It was extremely important that I didn't leave anything or anyone out. The wording had to be perfect. I spent a very long time getting his obituary just right.

An old friend from high school was his only visitor that afternoon. I welcomed Bill's company and the distraction that he provided, as it had been very quiet and I'd completed Jerry's obituary and tucked away in my purse. Bill and I visited quietly for an hour or so. I wiped Jerry's face and nose frequently, which was necessary due to the shutting down of his organs. I also checked his legs discreetly as one nurse had showed me how to look for "lacing," which was a subtle sign that Jerry's circulation was slowly down. The lacing on Jerry's legs became more pronounced every time I looked at them

At about 3:00 in the afternoon, Jerry's brother and father came into the room, and I excused myself. I was going to drive forty minutes home to wait for Danny to get out of soccer practice and his team dinner and return with him to see his father. I had texted the boys during the day, explaining that their dad was peaceful and that I thought they'd like to see him this way, rather than leave the previous day's images etched in their memories. Phillip declined the offer, but Danny said that he wanted to see his dad that evening.

When I got home, I took Phillip to my mother's house, which is around the corner from ours. My sister and niece, Tricia, were there and were going to stay to eat with Mom and Phillip. I promised to keep everyone updated and left quickly so I could go home and vacuum a little before Danny got home. Even a small task such as vacuuming gave me the feeling of control during this very chaotic time.

While I was vacuuming, I heard a loud knock at my front wooden door. It was my neighbor, Toni. She had heard the vacuum and knew that she'd have to knock loudly in order for me hear her. I welcomed her in, and she immediately asked how things were going. She's an administrative nurse and had heard, through the medical grapevine, that Jerry's illness had advanced quickly, but she wanted to be sure that she had been given accurate information. I appreciated her concern. While I was in the middle of replaying the events of the past week, my cell phone rang. I looked at the caller ID and recognized my brother-in-law's name. I turned my head toward Toni and said flatly, "This isn't good."

"What's going on, Dom?"

"Nancy," he choked, "We lost him. Jerry died a few minutes ago."

"Damn it, Dom. I tried to be there! I sat there all week so he wouldn't die without me." And then I remembered telling Jerry that he could go when he needed to and he didn't have to worry about anything, that I'd finish the job that we'd started, meaning that I'd finish raising our sons in the same way that we had been doing it together.

Toni was already standing next to me waiting to hold me in her arms when I got off the phone. I told Dom that I'd get to the hospital as soon as I could. I asked him not to let them take Jerry away until I got there.

After crying for just a moment, I made Toni promise not to tell a soul that Jerry had died, because Danny wouldn't know until he got home, and I wanted my mother or sister to tell him. She promised to keep it to herself until later that evening, and then I left my house quickly. I drove to my mother's house. When I walked in, everyone looked at me, wondering why I had come back so soon. "Did you change your mind? Do you want to eat with us?" my sister asked.

Phillip's eyes connected with mine, and he knew. "I'm so sorry, sweetie. I'm so sorry. It's over. Dad is gone."

Strangely, everyone seemed shocked. Everyone, that is, except Phillip. He fell into my arms and we held each other for a long time, and I asked him if he wanted to come to the hospital with me to see his dad this last time. Again, he declined. I left my sister and mother with the terrible task of having to tell Danny when he returned home from his team dinner that his father was dead. I didn't have time to wait for him. I had to get back to the hospital before they moved Jerry's body.

History

"History, despite its wrenching pain, cannot
be unlived, but if faced with courage, need
not be lived again."—Maya Angelou

Three and a half years before, it had been my heartbreaking
task, shared with my brother and sister-in-law, to tell my
sister that her husband of twenty-seven years had been
killed instantly in a car accident. The sheriff offered to
do it, but we felt that it would be terribly frightening for
Joan to walk into a room without suspecting a thing,
only to have a sheriff—a total stranger—tell her that Jim
had died that morning. Mike, Mary, and I told her in the
faculty lounge at the school where she teaches. I hated
being one of the three to tell her the worst news she'd ever
gotten in her life. I still feel a tremendous amount of guilt
about it today. Guilt is a terrible burden to bear. I can't
explain why I felt guilt more than any other emotion. Joan
has told me dozens of times that she would have much
rather been informed of Jim's accident by loved ones than
by the police, but the guilt has never really gone away.

Guilt stays with you like a scar. The actual injury is what physically and emotionally hurts you, but the scar remains a constant reminder of that terrible day. That scar remains on my heart, a constant reminder of the day I obliterated my sister's faith in life.

I used to read the book *The Devil's Arithmetic* by Jane Yolen with my sixth grade students every year. In the book, a young girl has been thrust into life as a Jewish prisoner, attempting to survive in a concentration camp. She compares the horrors of this existence to, "living in the belly of the wolf." Every time I read that paragraph, I'd get chills up and down my spine. I couldn't fathom anything being so terrible that it would seem as if you were residing in the belly of a wolf. The day that Jim died, while riding in the backseat of my brother's car on our way to deliver the awful news, I had a moment of clarity: *This is what being in the belly of the wolf feels like.* I had never been so terrified of the unknown in my life. We had no way of knowing how Joan would react, nor did we know how the day would unfold and how the events would change our lives forever.

Good-bye

"Death is more universal than life; everyone
dies but not everyone lives."—A. Sachs

I didn't speed to the hospital; there was absolutely no
reason to rush. I had missed the biggest event of my
husband's life ... his last breath. All the way there, I kept
saying out loud, "My husband is dead. I am a widow.
My children don't have a father anymore." From the van,
I called the funeral home director that I had been in
contact with during the past week to inform him that
Jerry had died and that his body would need to be picked
up later that evening. Jerry wanted to be cremated and
that couldn't be done over the weekend, so the funeral
arrangements were going to be a bit delayed.

When I was within a minute or so of arriving at the
hospital, I called my friend, Lori, who, sadly, had lost her
precious son, John Robert a few years earlier to sudden
infant death syndrome. I knew that she'd understand that
I just needed to say the words.

"Hi, Nance. What's up? Is everything okay?" Lori

asked tentatively. She knew. Undoubtedly she knew, but she didn't want to ask the obvious question, "Did Jerry die?"

"He's gone, Lor. Jerry died a little while ago. I just had to say it because I don't believe it." Lori expressed her sympathy, and I told her that I'd be in contact with her the next day. I then walked into F. F. Thompson Hospital to see my husband for the last time.

My brother and sister-in-law had called me while I was driving to the hospital to ask if they could come to the hospital to say good-bye to Jerry. It's funny, when I think of it—we said good-bye all week, yet there never seemed to be enough good-byes. No one was satisfied with the number of good-byes we had been given except maybe Phillip. For him, there were too many good-byes.

I got off of the elevator on the third floor, walked past the nurses' station without acknowledging any of them and into Jerry's quiet hospital room. His father and brother were sitting solemnly in chairs not far from Jerry's bed, simply looking sadly at their departed son and brother. I walked past them, nodding my head in acknowledgment, and went right to Jerry.

Superman

I know my kingdom awaits
and they've forgiven my mistakes
I'm coming home, I'm coming home
tell the world I'm coming

P.Diddy

"Well, Superman, you did it. I hope you're in Tennessee right now, at Fleming's Steak House, eating a beautiful steak dinner." I touched Jerry's arms, his face, and his chest. I wanted to remember his skin. Jerry had remarkably smooth arms and beautiful skin. It's strange to think of someone who died from skin cancer as having beautiful skin, but he really did.

Dom described the moment of Jerry's death to me with difficulty. He told me that Jerry's father had just walked out of his room to check on a relative who visited every day but sat in the visitor's lounge. Cousin David loved Jerry dearly but couldn't stand to see him suffer, so he did a sort of vigil, sitting for hours a day in the lounge to be close by to his cousin without actually being in the same room with him. Dom said that he was sitting next to Jerry when he made a strange sound, a different breath from the others. A nurse, Anne, was standing at the door, looking over paperwork before coming into the room to check on Jerry. Dom looked back at her, afraid of what was happening.

"I think something is happening. Can you come here?"

"He's leaving," Anne explained. "He's dying," she clarified.

And then Anne did a very loving thing. She did exactly what I would have done if I had been there. She stroked Jerry's arm, placed her hand on his forehead, and said, "It's okay, Jerry. You can let go now."

That was Jerry's last breath. He let go that quickly and easily, less than two hours after I left the hospital to pick up Danny. My husband died in the presence of his big brother.

Later, when Dom was describing the emotional difficulty he experienced as a result of witnessing Jerry's death, I said, "You know, Dom, I'm sure that it's hard for you to have this memory, but I think there's something beautiful about the fact that Jerry came into this world with his big brother in his life and left this world with his big brother by his side." Dom nodded his head, not really agreeing with me. It was simply too painful a memory to carry for the rest of his life.

We all stayed as long as we needed to. And then, when it was clearly time to leave, I was able to walk away because I had two sons at home waiting for me. I had always tried to make things better for them, to fix things when they went wrong. I was not going to be able to fix their father's illness and death. They had lived through a terrible four months, watching as their father's health declined and he became another person. There were going to be hard days to come, and I needed to be with them, to help them through it. I simply walked over to a small floral arrangement on the window sill that had arrived the day before, picked it up, slid it in the garbage, and walked away after kissing my husband good-bye.

Everybody Knew

The texts and phone calls began immediately. My brother drove my van for me, allowing me to relax and not worry about driving safely. My sister called to ask if we were on our way home; the boys were concerned about me.

Friends and family members texted short messages of support and love. I appreciated every one of them but couldn't fathom how word had spread so quickly. Danny took his Dad's cell phone that night and read the many text messages that came from Jerry's friends. Most of them said something like, "RIP, friend. I'll miss you." Danny still has his father's phone, and we have saved all of those messages. It took me months after Jerry's death to build up the emotional courage to read those texts. I still wonder if Jerry had any idea how much his friends loved him.

Just like the night that I drove home from Strong Memorial Hospital and left Jerry in the emergency room with a preliminary diagnosis of cancer, I came home to find my family in my house waiting to support me. They had been there for my sons before I arrived. Danny and

Phillip met me at the door and hugged me, and we cried openly together. They told me that they'd called Jerry's two best friends from work because they didn't want Fred and Brian to hear about Jerry's death from anyone but them. I'm sure that these two men were proud to think that the boys had the sense of responsibility to think of others at this painful time. I was certainly proud of their maturity and courage.

The boys asked me a little later if they could contact some friends with the news. They needed to do exactly as I had done when I called Lori; they needed to say it out loud: "My father is dead. I don't have a father anymore." It makes it real when you say it out loud. Of course, I told them, "Yes, you can start telling your friends and they are welcome at our house or at Grandma's to visit you during the next few days. You're going to need your friends."

Nobody stayed too long. We were all exhausted and needed to sleep. The next several days were going to be long and hard, and we all needed to go home and mentally prepare for them.

Phillip ... My Hero

My sister told me four months after Jerry died that she had been waiting at my house with her daughter, Tricia, and Phillip to tell Danny, when he returned from practice that day, but Phillip had stepped up to the plate instead. When Danny's truck pulled into the driveway Joan said, "Phillip, I'll tell Danny, Honey. I can do this."

Phillip replied, "No, he should hear it from me." He walked to the door, opened it for his brother and said, "It's over, Danny. Dad is gone." I'll never find the words to express how impressed I am with my son. I'm so touched that he found the strength to tell his brother this heartbreaking news. I don't think he'll ever know the deep impression that has made on me. He is such a strong, brave soul.

Days of Nothingness

"You must do the thing you think you cannot do."—Eleanor Roosevelt

The next day was Saturday and funeral arrangements had to be made. The night before, the mortician had picked up Jerry's body and brought it to the funeral home. Danny wanted to help me plan his father's calling hours and funeral. Phillip chose not to be involved in this process. Phillip had been invited to play in a basketball tournament with some of his friends, and we all agreed that he should do as many of his "normal" activities as possible in the days leading up to the funeral. Danny would be faced with the task of playing in a sectional soccer game later that Saturday. As I mentioned earlier, Danny was a captain on his high school's soccer team, and they were about to play their last sectional game. Danny wouldn't have even considered not playing.

Danny and I had brought some pictures, hats, a lacrosse stick, and other personal items of Jerry's that we wanted displayed during the calling hours. Before we walked into the funeral home, Danny stopped and turned to me and asked, "Mom, is Dad here?" I realized that he was concerned about actually seeing his father's body. I think the boys had been relieved when I told them days earlier that Jerry wanted to be cremated. I stopped and told Danny that, yes, his father's body was in the building, but that we wouldn't see it. He'd be in another location in the funeral home. Later, the funeral director asked us if we wanted to see Jerry, but we both declined. I saw Jerry for the last time the night before, and Danny had no need to see his father's body. I'm sure that he wanted to start trying to remember his father as the happy-go-lucky man that he had been before cancer took over.

The process of planning a funeral can be lengthy, but Danny and I are decisive people, so it didn't take any longer than necessary. I had already written Jerry's obituary, and I had a beautiful photograph of him that I wanted printed with it. Danny's opinion meant a great deal to me. He was allowed to overrule me on some aspects, such as the prayer cards, the acknowledgment cards, and the cover of the guest sign-in book. I didn't want him to think that I had agreed to his help only to do everything myself. The calling hours would be on Wednesday and Jerry's funeral would be on Thursday. Tuesday, the day before calling hours, was my forty-seventh birthday. Jerry had remembered it briefly the last week of his life. He said, one day at the hospital, "You have a birthday next week." I had made light of it because I felt pretty certain that he wouldn't be alive to see this birthday. I told him that we'd celebrate my birthday when he came home from the hospital.

After we made all the funeral arrangements, I dropped

Danny off at home and went downtown to choose floral arrangements from me and the boys. I wanted Jerry to have bright, colorful flowers for two reasons: first, he deserved to be surrounded by nothing but beauty; and second, I wanted the flowers to distract from the urn that contained Jerry's cremains. I hoped that it would be, somehow, less painful to see the urn sitting on the table if there were flowers all around it to distract everyone from the reality of what was inside the urn.

I didn't attend Danny's sectional soccer game that night. It was too far from home, and I couldn't leave my mother's house where all of our friends had gathered to pay their respects. His team lost the game, but there was a very nice article in the newspaper the next day about how the team had played well considering the loss of one of their greatest supporters, Jerry Galusha, the father of team captain and senior, Danny Galusha.

There were, in my opinion, too many days of nothingness between Jerry's death and his calling hours and funeral. People dropped off enormous amounts of food and drink. They also brought toilet paper, napkins, cups, plastic ware, and paper towels. It was all very kind and generous, but it was too much. Although we appreciated it, no family can possibly eat or use everything that is sent during a time of bereavement. I eventually turned down people who called to ask if they could bring something over. "No, please. We have too much now as it is," I pleaded with well-wishers on the phone. After the funeral was over and everyone went back to their normal routines, we ended up calling our local food pantry and donating anything that they could take to put on their shelves. They gladly accepted baked goods and perishable foods for their break room. We were happy to share these treats with people who appreciated them instead of just throwing them in the garbage.

Even the flowers and plants became far too much to discard discreetly. My entire front porch was full of floral arrangements and plants. A UPS delivery man arrived late in the afternoon on the day of Jerry's funeral. He looked at me and then at the rain forest on my porch, and I asked, "Do you have a girlfriend or a wife?"

"Yeah," he responded.

"Wouldn't you like to take some flowers or a plant to her tonight?"

He considered it seriously and then, I believe, out of good taste, declined my offer. In the end, my sister-in-law's mother took most of the plants. She has a green thumb, and I was very grateful that I didn't have to throw them all away. The neighbors would have seen the very plants that they had spent a great deal of money on stuffed in my garbage can that Sunday night. I hated the thought of offending anyone.

My First Jerry-less Birthday

November 9 marked my forty-seventh birthday. My poor family! What a lousy job it was to "celebrate" my birthday while at the same time trying to accept the loss of our cherished Jerry. In the end, we all had dinner together at my mother's house, ate a cake that someone had dropped off, and I opened very generous, expensive gifts. They went overboard in trying to compensate for my loss. It was so kind of them. I received, as a gift from my brother, sister, and sister-in-law, my first and only pair of UGG boots—an extravagance I would have never afforded myself.

Calling Hours

The next day, Wednesday, November 10, 2010, we stood in line at Doran Funeral Home for six hours hugging people and thanking them for their support. The calling hours were supposed to be from 4:00 p.m. to 8:00 p.m., but so many people were lined up outside of the funeral home by 3:00 that we had to open the doors and let them start coming through. We didn't leave the funeral home until close to 10:00 p.m. that night. My feet were numb after the first two hours. Danny wouldn't leave my side, but Phillip hated standing in line. After about an hour, he wandered off. He meandered around the funeral home, talking to friends and family members in the hallway and in the other rooms. Phillip is very social, and being able to speak with family and friends on his own terms was a better option for him. Family members brought us bottles of water and suggested that we take a bathroom break or sit for a while, but, honestly, the line of well-wishers wouldn't slacken enough for us to be able to do either. The priest hadn't planned to give a final prayer that night, because we still had the funeral to attend the next day, but I finally told him that the only way I thought people would get the idea that it was time for us to leave was if he offered a prayer—a signal that we literally couldn't stay there any longer.

Our Last Day with Jerry

I've been early for every major event of my life. Jerry's funeral was no exception. But when we pulled up in front of the church, I panicked. There wasn't a parking spot to be found; people were already entering the church while others milled around on the sidewalk waiting for their friends and family so they could enter as a group. The boys and I got out of the car that my nephew Greg was driving for us and walked into the church. Even though we were easily twenty minutes early, it looked like there wasn't a seat left in our very large Catholic church. It was Veteran's Day, and most people had the day off from work, so more people than usual were able to attend Jerry's weekday funeral. Because the boys and I sat in the very first pew, and I didn't look back during the funeral mass, I never really knew how full the church became. People later told me that there were people standing in the aisles because there were no more seats. Jerry wouldn't have believed the crowd that he had drawn.

I personally believe that at that time, the boys and I were just grateful that Jerry's pain had ended, so we weren't emotional at his funeral. Out of the three of us, I think I was the only one who teared up once, and that was because Danny eulogized his father so beautifully. Danny spoke of his father's calloused hands, telling the crowd that his father had always said that he didn't want his sons to have to work as physically hard as he had. It was always Jerry's dream to have his sons attend college and work in professions as opposed to the physical labor that Jerry had always performed. Months later, it wouldn't take much of anything for any of us to cry at the drop of a hat. In Wal-Mart one day, I found myself reaching for a can of black olives and dissolved into tears. No one in the house liked olives except Jerry. I no longer had any reason to buy olives.

After Danny spoke of his father's legacy, a friend from elementary school, Jill, also spoke about Jerry at his funeral. She did an exemplary job sharing stories about Jerry's fun and quirky character. Jerry had been all boy as a youngster and often did naughty things, just for the thrill. For instance, Jerry wanted to make some extra money when he was in seventh grade at our tiny Catholic school. He went to the drugstore downtown and bought a bottle of cinnamon extract and a few boxes of toothpicks. Jerry spent an entire day dipping the toothpicks into the cinnamon extract to make cinnamon flavored toothpicks to sell at school for five cents each. Now, that alone doesn't sound so bad, except that he sold some of his toothpicks to a classmate who, unknowingly, was allergic to cinnamon. That toothpick sale resulted in an emergency trip to the hospital to bring Rich's swollen throat and eyes under control. Jerry also once blew up a rocket without his parents' permission. Unfortunately, the rocket malfunctioned. The explosion took off Jerry's eyebrows, his eyelashes, and most of the hair toward the front of his head. How Jerry lived through his childhood was anybody's guess.

One of my favorite stories about Jerry that wasn't told at his funeral was when his mother left a two-year-old Jerry home with his father on a Saturday afternoon. His dad worked nights and needed to sleep during the day, so he nodded off, assuming that Jerry would be fine as long as he was in the house and close by. His father must have slept more soundly than he realized, because Jerry toddled outside, down the porch, across the street, over a railroad track, through a parking lot, and into the little neighborhood grocery store. Jerry's father was awakened by the telephone ringing and the question, "Do you have a little boy about two years old?" Someone who worked in the store recognized Jerry, because he went to the store frequently with his mother. They called his father to report that Jerry was in the store, had torn open bags of candy, and was eating heartily while his father napped.

There were moments of genuine laughter at Jerry's funeral, which he would have loved. But the time came to end the funeral and bring Jerry's cremains to the cemetery. Jerry was to be buried next to his cherished brother-in-law, Jim. I don't really remember much about being at the cemetery except when the service ended I looked over to my right and saw Rick and Missy M. standing at their son Freddy's grave, a little distance from Jerry's, crying. Missy's face and nose were red as tears streamed down her face. Freddy had only been thirteen when he died unexpectedly the April before Jerry's death of a staph infection that spread, seemingly, at the speed of light.

Freddy was to have been on Phillip's baseball team, but he never got a chance to step foot on the field that spring, dying just before the opening of the season. Jerry had taken Freddy's death exceptionally hard; wondering what God could possibly need from a precious thirteen-year-old boy enough to take him away from his loving family. I walked over to Missy, hugged her, and told her that Jerry and Freddy wouldn't want us to stand at their graves and cry. It was easy for me to say then, but I've done it countless times myself since Jerry's death. I just wasn't far enough into my grief journey at that time to understand the lingering pain that this grief was going to take me through. Of course, I had lost my father, my mother-in-law, and my brother-in-law, but losing Jerry was very different; he was the father of my children.

The Last Supper

After the cemetery service, the boys and I went home quickly so they could change out of their dress clothes and into more comfortable attire. We were having a luncheon at a nearby restaurant so everyone could gather one last time and have a bite to eat before going back to their normal lives. Our lives wouldn't feel normal for a very long time … if ever … but I knew that everyone else's would, and this all had to come to an end soon. We were exhausted, and our world had been turned upside down. The time had come to start dealing with Jerry's absence.

One hundred and eighty-one people attended the luncheon after Jerry's funeral. Jerry's father's former boss, who owns a successful bowling alley, was extraordinarily generous and paid for all of the expenses, including an open bar. To this day, I have no idea what it cost, as I wasn't allowed to see the bill, but I'm very grateful for the kindness and generosity of the Malcuria family.

Our New Normal

The boys went back to school the next day, but I took that day and the following week off to put paperwork together, make phone calls, deliver death certificates to our banks, and go to the Social Security office. I found that one of our checking accounts had been automatically frozen due to Jerry's death. That was an unpleasant surprise. I tried my best not to be too rude about it, but it angered me. It was embarrassing to be standing at the checkout counter at the store and be told that my debit card had been deactivated. It was inconvenient and, in my opinion, unnecessary. The least they could have done was call me to tell me that their policy was to freeze the account until a death certificate was made available. Luckily, my other bank did not have the same policy, and I was able to use that ATM card.

I was instructed to get to the Social Security office as soon as possible with our birth certificates, Jerry's death certificate, and our social security cards. It takes time to get Social Security benefits up and running. Under our circumstances, the boys were entitled to a benefit check once a month, but Danny would only receive his for seven months. Once a dependent has graduated from high school or turns eighteen years old, his or her benefits end. Suddenly, the reality of losing Jerry's income and only getting benefits for Danny for seven more months was something I had to face and very seriously. I made decisions about what to do with life insurance money and Jerry's retirement death benefit based on trying to spend as little money per month as possible. I paid off all our debts, including credit cards and loans.

Possessions

Jerry had a truck that he adored. He'd only bought it a year and a half before his death. We actually had to park the truck at my mother's house during Jerry's illness because it was a terrible tease for him to look out at the driveway and see his truck parked there without being able to drive it. Jerry's oncologist had been very stern and had told Jerry that he was not permitted to drive under any circumstances, because of the amount of medication he was taking and his poor reaction time. The truck also took up a large amount of space in our driveway, and with the number of visitors in and out each day, we found that we needed the extra room in the driveway. I called the loan company to ask what to do with the truck. Although I'd offered to pay off the loan and buy the truck for Danny, he declined the offer stating the facts: it was expensive, it cost too much to fuel, and it was Dad's, not his. I respected his logic and had the truck voluntarily repossessed. It sounded harsh, but in reality it was a simple decision to make. I didn't want the truck, I didn't need the truck, and I didn't have the time or energy to figure out what it would take to sell a truck that Jerry still owed money on.

Having the truck towed away was the first thing that I had to do after Jerry's death that really hurt. I couldn't begin to cope with watching it be towed from our driveway, so we kept it at my mother's, and *she* had to witness the departure of the truck. I felt terrible that she had to go through the emotions associated with watching something that Jerry had loved so dearly being towed away as if it were no longer useful, and I appreciated her willingness to take that hit for us.

The gentleman that I spoke to on the phone made it all sound so easy. They would arrive at my mother's house, tow the truck, and we'd be finished with that business. In reality, it wasn't nearly that simple. After the truck was gone, I received a letter outlining the process that the truck would undertake. It would be sold at auction on December 2. If it sold for less than we owed, I would be responsible for paying the balance of the loan and the auction and towing fees associated with this transaction. If the truck sold for more than we owed, I would receive a check for the balance after the auction and towing fees were paid. Of course, I knew better than to believe that I'd actually make money on this deal, but I put it out of my mind and decided to cross that bridge when we got to it. A month or so later, I received a letter informing me that I owed over three thousand dollars to settle up on the truck. Luckily my name was not on the truck's loan, and, in the end, my lawyer informed the loan company that I was not responsible for paying anything for the truck. Jerry had the loan on the truck, not me, and there was no estate. Done deal.

We didn't have large life insurance policies on each other, but the one that we did have was acceptable to help me financially for a while. Jerry had a death benefit on his New York State retirement, so on paper it looked like I had a decent chunk of money available to me. In truth, over three-fourths of the death benefit had to go into an IRA, so it couldn't be taxed. And in order to make the house sellable, I would need to finish some large home repairs that Jerry and I had been working on. A large, expensive drainage job had to be completed in my basement. It was something that should have been done at least five years before, but it had been too expensive for us to consider. I also needed to have new vinyl siding put on the house. My house was a distasteful mint green color that I knew would turn potential buyers away. Eventually I replaced all of our fifty-year-old windows, had some of the hardwood refinished, replaced a sliding glass door, and did a lot of painting with the help of a friend who was very generous with his time.

The Firsts

As tough as I appeared on the outside, I was suffering on the inside. I had a hard time getting through day-to-day activities without Jerry. I hated going home on Friday afternoons. The house was empty, and the hustle and bustle of the weekdays was absent on the weekends. I missed Jerry all the more on the weekends. Friends were wonderful and tried to lure me out with promises of a good time, but I didn't want a good time; I wanted my old life back, and that life included my husband. Sadly, I knew that I'd have to accept that life goes forward, not backward. I grieved for my former life as much as I did for my deceased husband.

The firsts came fast and furiously. Thanksgiving was only a couple of weeks after Jerry died, and Christmas and the New Year followed quickly thereafter. Danny's eighteenth birthday was January 27. I tried to change things up in order to not notice Jerry's absence, as if that were really possible. Phillip happened to be away in Florida with a friend on Danny's birthday, but I treated our family to a pleasant lunch out at an unfamiliar restaurant instead of having a birthday celebration at home as I normally would have done.

Probably one of the hardest things to do was to contemplate the beginning of the baseball and lacrosse seasons. Danny's first lacrosse game was played at Aquinas Institute in Rochester on a cold, sunny Saturday in March. The game went well even though we lost by a single goal. Danny played a fantastic game, and it was the most competitive game that we'd ever played against the strong Bath-Haverling team, in the four years that Danny had played on the varsity lacrosse team. I was excited to meet up with my son when the game ended so I could congratulate him on winning most of his face-offs and playing such a great game. The minute I spotted Danny coming through the gates, I knew that he was in tremendous emotional pain. He was sobbing and came right into my arms. He cried openly and kept repeating, "I miss Dad, Mom. I miss him so much." Even his senior ball the night before hadn't been as difficult as his first lacrosse game of the season without his father, the man who had introduced Danny to the sport of lacrosse.

Shortly thereafter, we faced the first home game of the lacrosse season. This would be the first time that I would pull into the familiar parking lot and not look for Jerry's truck. He almost always drove separately from me because he usually came straight from work or running errands. On this particular evening, the team had planned a moment of silence for Jerry, and I was miserable thinking about the sad tone with which the team would begin the season. To add to the emotions, another Mynderse Academy lacrosse patriarch had died unexpectedly that week, so many people attended this particular game to show their support for the program and of the families who'd lost their loved ones. Boys and girls of all ages lined the field wearing their lacrosse jerseys and lowered their heads after memories of Jerry and Al H. were read over the loudspeaker. Phillip sat next to me and put his arm around me during this time of respect for his dad. He refused to cry in public, but I could tell that he was having a hard time keeping his emotions together.

I was glad when that moment was over and I could just be a lacrosse mom, sitting in the bleachers, attending her son's game. Danny played remarkably well, winning fourteen of his eighteen face-offs that night, scoring one goal and assisting others—all while wearing the number twenty-two in honor of his father. Danny had worn the number one for as long as it had been available while he was on the varsity team, but during this, his senior year, he wanted to wear his father's former lacrosse number, and the player who had staked claim to the number twenty-two jersey kindly gave it up for Danny without any hesitation. It was such a kind and thoughtful thing to do. Aaron P. will always be a very special young man to me for giving up his jersey number for Danny that season.

A Playground by Any Other Name

"She stood in the storm and when the wind did not blow her away, she adjusted her sails."—Elizabeth Edwards

A couple of months after Jerry died, the director of our community center, Jim S., asked me if it would be okay if they dedicated the new playground in Seneca Falls to Jerry. It was a tremendous honor, and, of course, I said yes. Jerry had worked so very hard on that playground. He initially signed up to work two hours on it, but, as always seemed to be the case where Jerry's volunteer work was concerned, once he got there he realized that two hours wasn't going to make a dent in this project. He spent what felt like countless hours rebuilding the existing playground over the course of several weekends. On May 22, 2011, the Jerry Galusha Memorial Playground was dedicated to my deceased husband. Many people attended the ceremony, including community members, family, friends, village employees, etc. When I spoke on behalf of Jerry, thanking our community for the honor of this dedication and for all that everyone had done to help us during the time of Jerry's illness, there wasn't a dry eye in the audience. This was to be, I promised myself, the one and only time that I was going to hang my head out there and publically speak about the time of Jerry's illness, so I had to be sure to do an above-average job.

The week or so leading up to the dedication ceremony was very difficult. I dreaded the emotions that were sure to erupt that day. I hated the thought of my sons hurting once again. Mostly, though, I dreaded standing in front of a large crowd, all by myself, and attempting to do justice to what everyone had done for us. I didn't sleep well, and I cried silently at night. I was profoundly miserable.

However, once the day came, I made up my mind that I'd do whatever I could, and everyone would have to accept that a grieving widow can't always be poised, polished, and articulate on the day of a playground dedication ceremony for her husband. In the end, I did just fine. I said everything that I felt really needed to be said, and I survived. It was hard to do, but I would have been furious with myself if I hadn't succeeded in my task. The playground itself is bittersweet. I envision my sons coming home to Seneca Falls to visit me with their families in the future and taking their children to "Grandpa's playground." We will have to tell those children about a grandfather that they will never know. I have a hard time getting my head around that.

New Drugs, New Sadness

In early June, 2011 news broke that two promising drugs were being tested in the fight against melanoma. I don't know why that news brought out the worst in me, but I had trouble sleeping that night. "If only," was the theme of that day. I couldn't believe that Jerry had died seven months shy of the opportunity to try those drugs. I try not to read articles about new drugs and medical advances now, because I know that the emotions attached to these medical updates just hurt me unnecessarily. That ship has sailed for us, and I hope I never need to rely on medical information about melanoma again in my lifetime.

Graduations

Although I had promised myself that the most difficult of the emotions were over, the very next month brought the planning and execution of my son's high school graduation—the very occasion that Jerry had tried so hard to live for. In trying not to change anything that had initially been planned, I rented the tent, ordered the food, bought the party supplies—all while wearing my brave face. Phillip's middle school moving-up ceremony was the night before Danny's graduation, so it was a double whammy, and it all hurt like hell. However, the day of Danny's graduation party, July 18, 2011, was a beautiful, sunny, warm day, and I was so busy I didn't really have much time to feel my emotions. It was a day of doing things instead of feeling them.

Danny Leaves Home

The day after the graduation party Danny, was scheduled to leave for his summer job at Camp Stella Maris in Livonia, NY. He lingered around the house longer than I expected him to, and, sensing that he was hesitant to leave, I asked him why he wasn't already on the road. With a catch in his voice, he spoke of his concerns: "I feel bad leaving you guys." Danny had always had a self-imposed sense of responsibility. I never told him that I needed him to stay home for the summer so the three of us could be together, to lick our wounds, but he felt that he should be home instead of away. I assured Danny that Phillip and I would be all right and that we'd see him on the weekends. What else could I do? He was committed to his summer job, and I knew that it would be the best thing for him. Danny had geared himself to work at this camp for years. I wasn't going to stand in his way.

Me, Phil, and Pain

Phillip and I then began a very difficult summer. Although neither of us had an all-out meltdown, it was obvious to me that Phillip was doing everything in his power to be home as little as possible. He spent almost every night at one friend's or another's. We had gone from being a family of four to a family of two, and our house didn't feel like a home. I tried to honor his need to remove himself from our home, where all of the emptiness existed, but I worried sick about him. By the end of the summer, I discovered a few minor behavioral issues that Philip had developed over the summer, and when I addressed them with Phil, he agreed to grief counseling.

Living in a Fish Bowl

I knew that grief counseling was the best thing for Phillip, but I have to admit that I worried that he'd expose all of my flaws to the counselor. In retrospect, I had nothing to worry about. Counseling lasted a few months, and when it concluded Phillip felt better and stronger. It was, without a doubt, the best decision we made. I'm very proud of Phillip's willingness to speak to a total stranger about his experiences and losses. As facts unraveled, he really dealt with the deaths of his grandfather (2001), his grandmother (2005), his uncle (2007), his friend Freddy (2010), and his father (2010). Think about it … that's a lot of losses for a fourteen-year-old boy! I was usually not invited into his counseling sessions. The sessions were intended for just Phil and the counselor, so I wasn't really privy to what they discussed. He never seemed upset when we left, so I had to assume that things were going well. But on the last day, the counselor invited me in. She surprised me by saying, "Phil, you and I have had a lot of great conversations, and you have told me some really nice things about your mom. Why don't you give your mom one example of something that she's done for you since your dad died that you really appreciate." Phillip told me how much he appreciated me letting him to go Florida with his friend James's family two months after Jerry died. He said that he would have understood if I hadn't wanted him to be that far away from home for several days but that he was really glad that I had allowed him to go. I left that appointment feeling like a success for the first time in a long time.

Two Long Years

November 5 will always be a sad day for me and the boys. It seemed like this year all three of us reacted to it even more harshly than last year. Danny called me the day before, November 4, and, with emotion in his voice, asked if he had the anniversary day correct. I told him that it was actually the following day, but as long as he'd spent half the day mourning, he might as well finish the day up and give himself a break the next day (Monday.) Phillip was exceptionally quiet on November 4 and 5 as well. Me? I try so hard to be a Pollyanna and tell everyone that we're fine, we're moving forward, and that it's just a day on the calendar, but, truth be told, I suffer on November 5 just as much as everyone else.

Jerry's buddy, Brian, goes to the cemetery and drinks a beer to "drown his sorrows" every year on November 5. This year, true to form, I found the empty beer can at Jerry's headstone the day after the anniversary of his death.

People told me that the second year of grieving would be even harder than the first, and they were correct. It felt as if my nerve endings were on fire at times. I anticipated the end of the second year with a positive attitude, thinking that the worst would be over but found the beginning of the third year pretty bad as well. I was crying at the drop of a hat and wasn't sleeping well. It took several weeks to get back on my feet. It seemed as though the feelings and emotions were as fresh as they had been in the days right after Jerry's untimely death.

Today

Danny is a sophomore in college at SUNY Fredonia, and Phillip is a sophomore in high school. I am still working at Seneca Falls Middle School. I appreciate that Phillip is busy with three sports a year, as it affords me a social life with the other athletes' parents and a purpose in my own life. I try not to think about the fact that he'll be leaving home in two and a half short years and that I'll be alone for the first time in twenty-five years.

The Future

"Fate is what happens to you. Destiny is
how you respond."—Jim Curtan

My future is now a blank canvas. I thought I'd be retiring and traveling south every winter with Jerry, living out our golden years. We looked forward to one day being grandparents. We were going to grow old together. My preconceived dreams died with Jerry on November 5, 2010. I don't doubt that new dreams will emerge. I have enough faith in God, in the world, and in myself to know that I will have a future and a good one at that. I've been asked by many how I can appear to be so positive, have so much faith in a world that, through the very thing that gives us light, warmth, and life, caused my husband's cancer … the sun. I don't have a canned answer. I can't quote a scripture that sums up my beliefs. All I can say is that throughout my husband's illness, upon his untimely death, and in the two years since, I have seen the best in people because I looked for it. I refuse to live a bitter life. If I'm bitter, then cancer won, and I won't allow cancer to beat me. The people of Seneca Falls, the people of Mynderse Academy, the people of the Midey, Blanchard, Galusha, Dreitlein, Fera, and Manzari families, the people of Sands Cancer Treatment Center, the people of F. F. Thompson Hospital, the people of Romulus Central School, the employees of the former Village of Seneca Falls—all of these wonderful people have given me the strength to move forward, a little bit every day. I still draw upon the love and support that I felt during my family's darkest days, and they have never failed me.

About the Author

Nancy A. Midey Galusha was born on November 9, 1963 in Seneca Falls, NY. She has an associate's degree in child development from the former Maria Regina College, a bachelor's degree from SUNY Cortland in elementary education, a master's degree from Elmira College in elementary education, and a Masters Degree from Mansfield University in school library and information technology. She taught elementary school for twenty-two years at Romulus Central School in Romulus, NY and began her library career in 2009 at Seneca Falls Middle School, Seneca Falls, NY. She is the mother of two sons: Daniel, twenty, who is a student at SUNY Fredonia; and Phillip, sixteen, who is a sophomore at Mynderse Academy, Seneca Falls, NY. She was married to Gerard "Jerry" Galusha for almost twenty years before he died of malignant melanoma at the age of forty-six on November 5, 2010. She resides with her sons in Seneca Falls, NY and enjoys reading, writing, being a mother, and attending her sons' school activities, especially soccer, basketball, baseball, and lacrosse games.